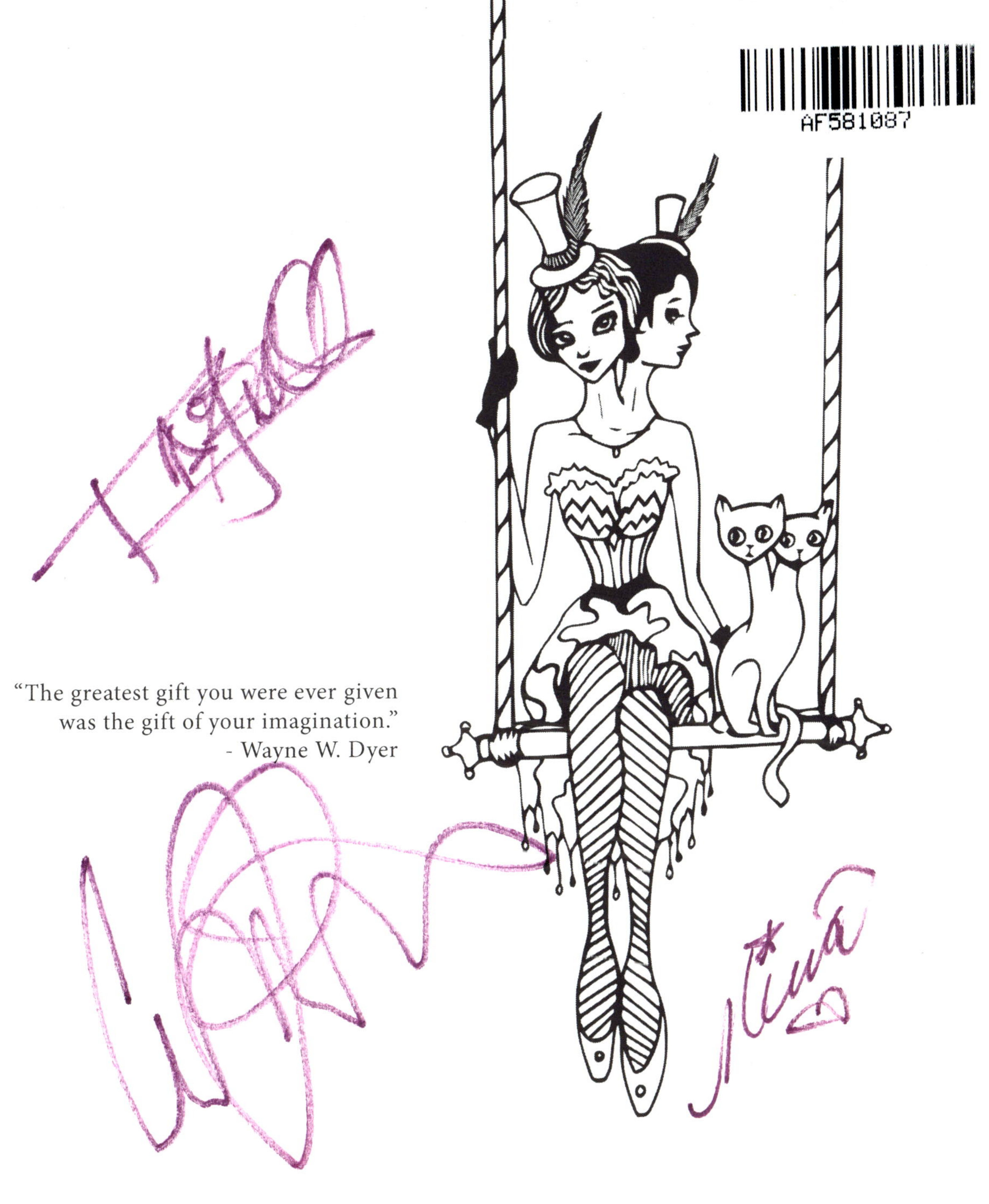

"The greatest gift you were ever given
was the gift of your imagination."
- Wayne W. Dyer

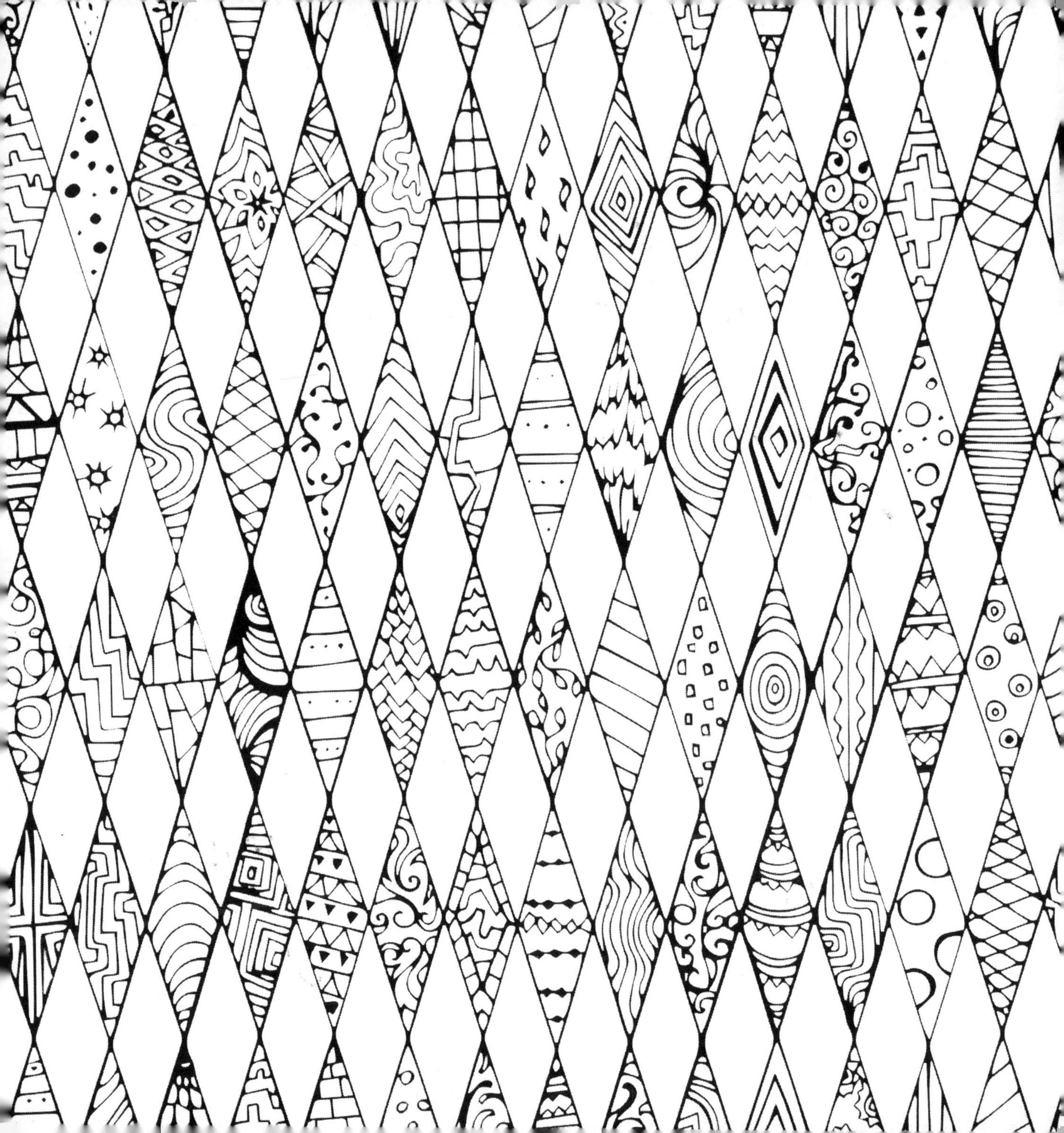

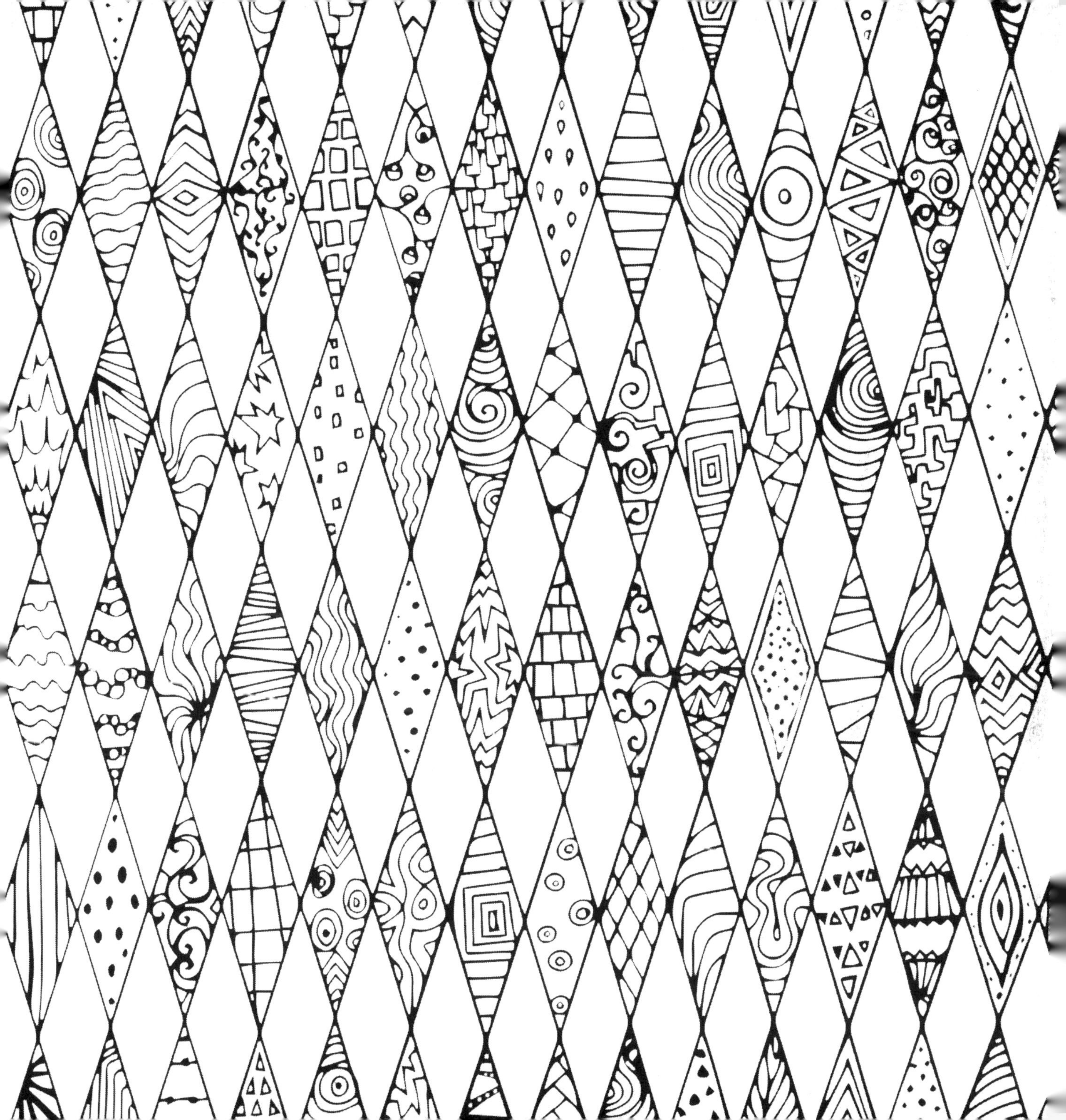

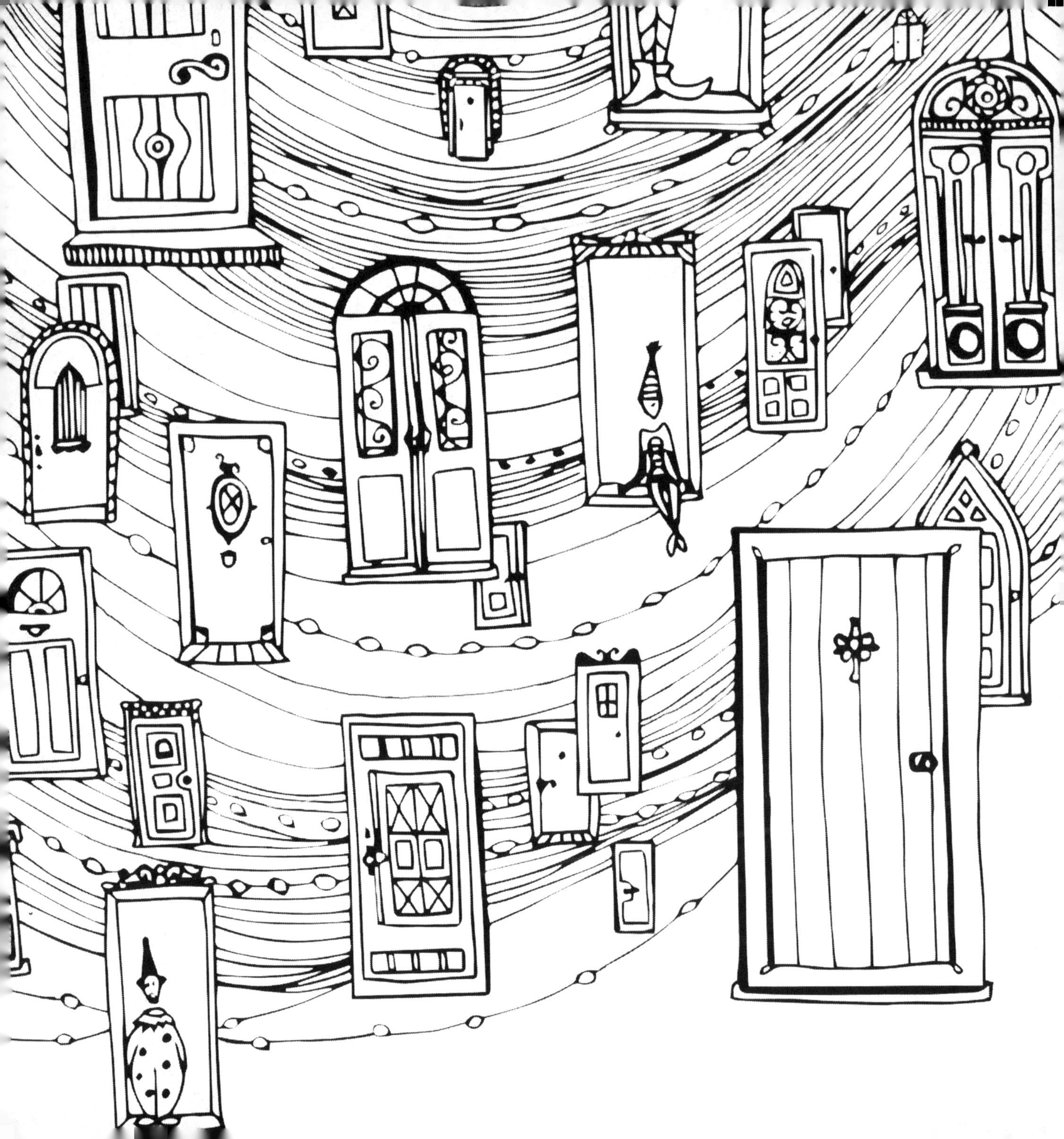

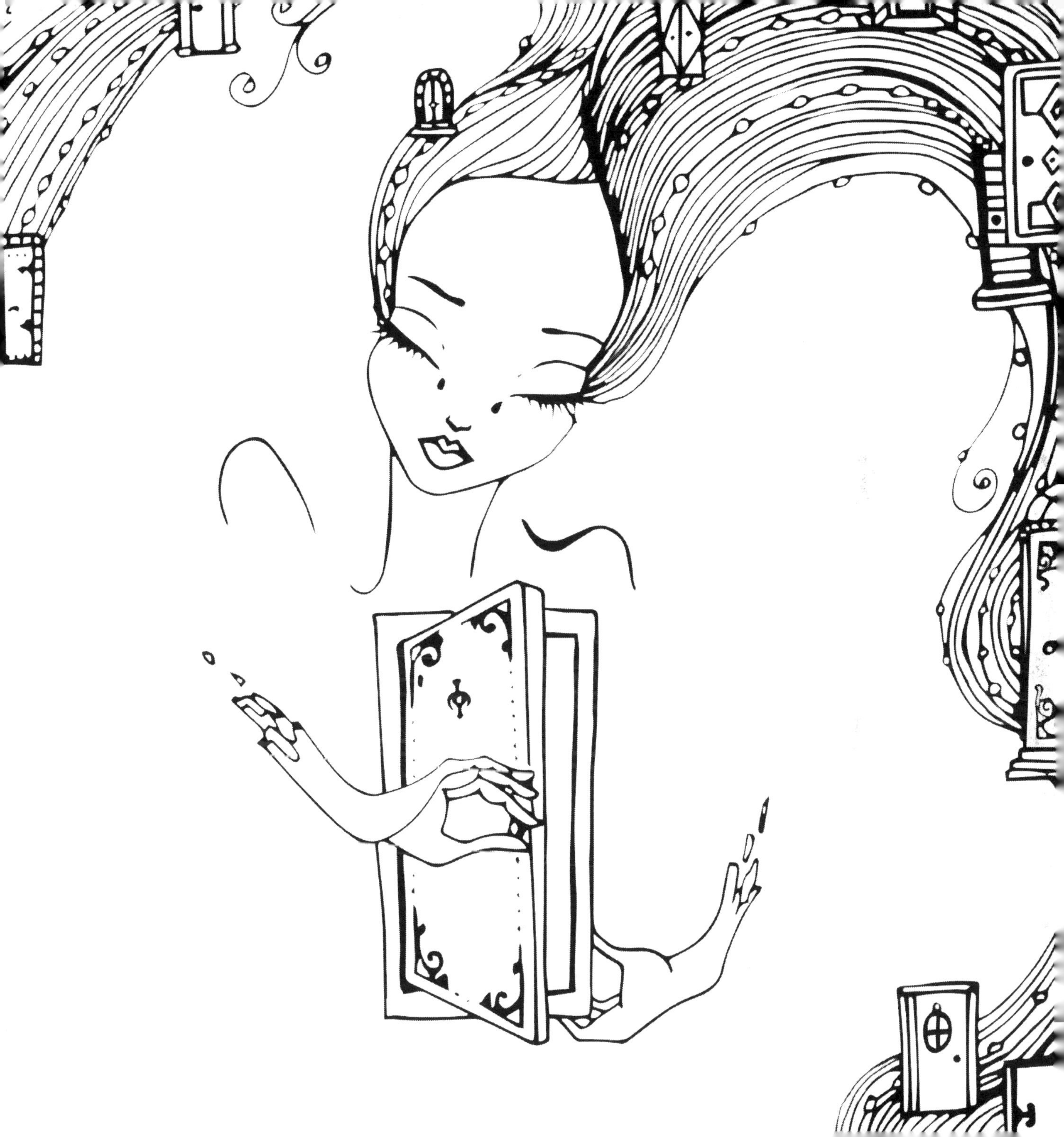

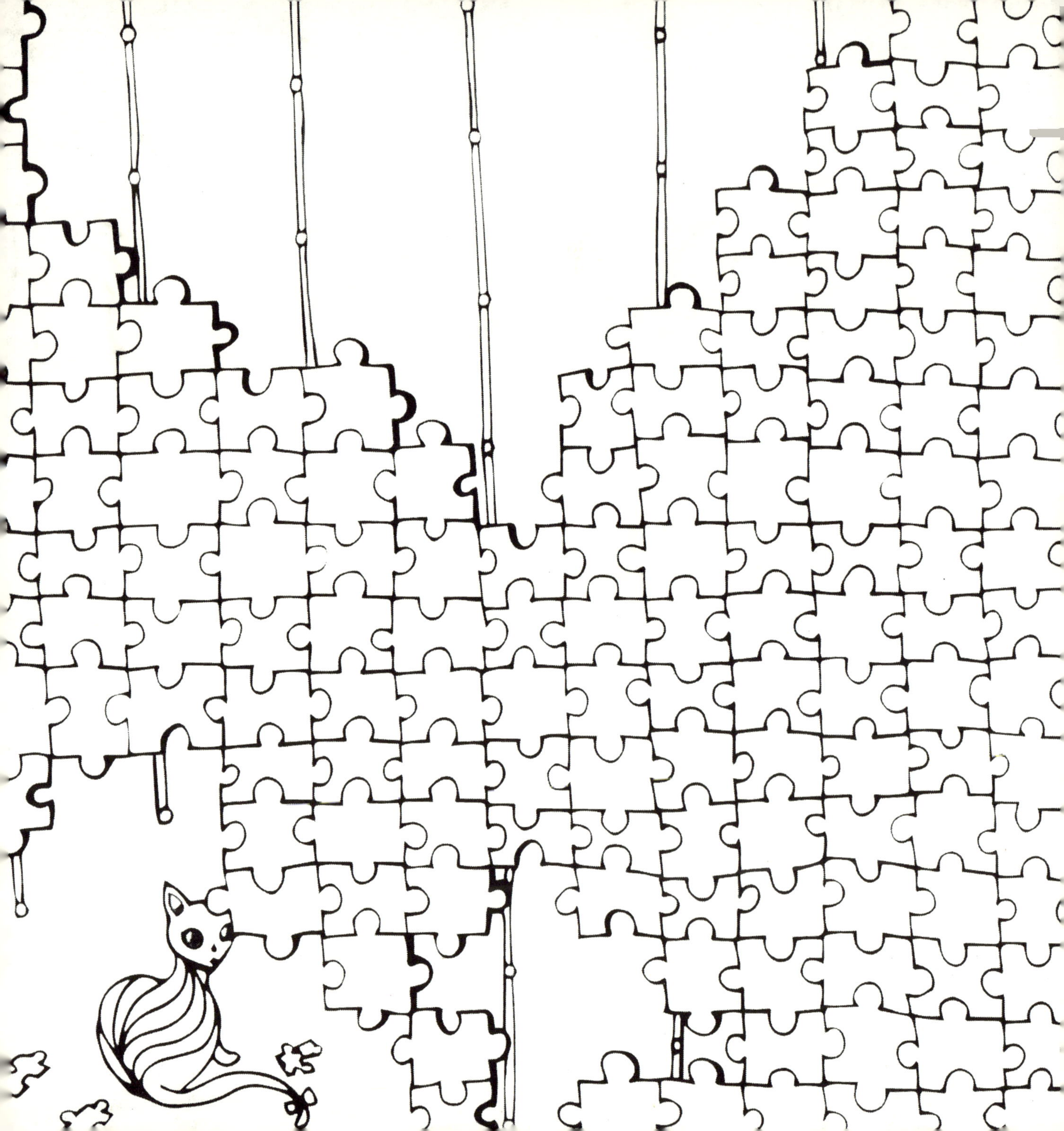

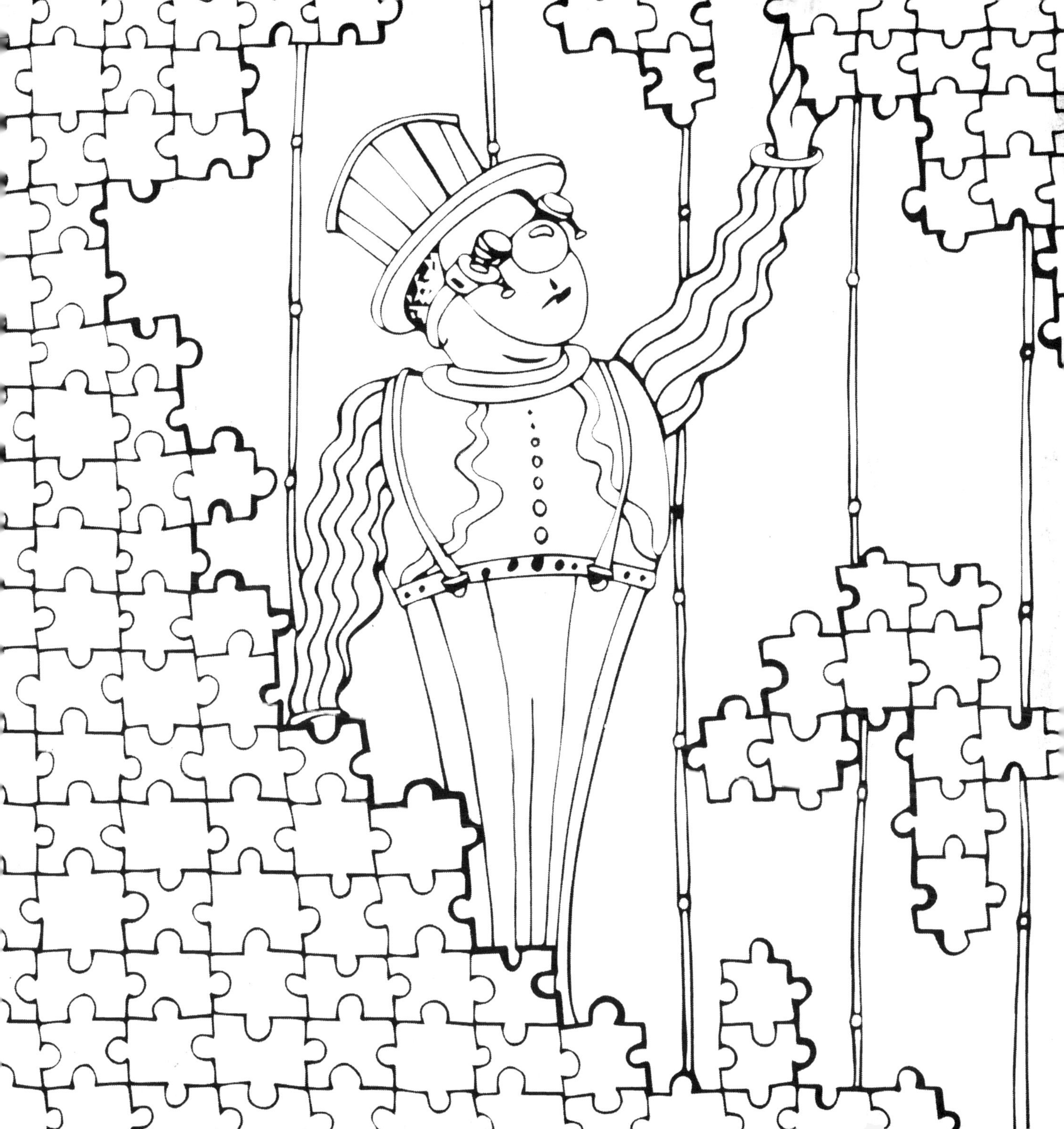

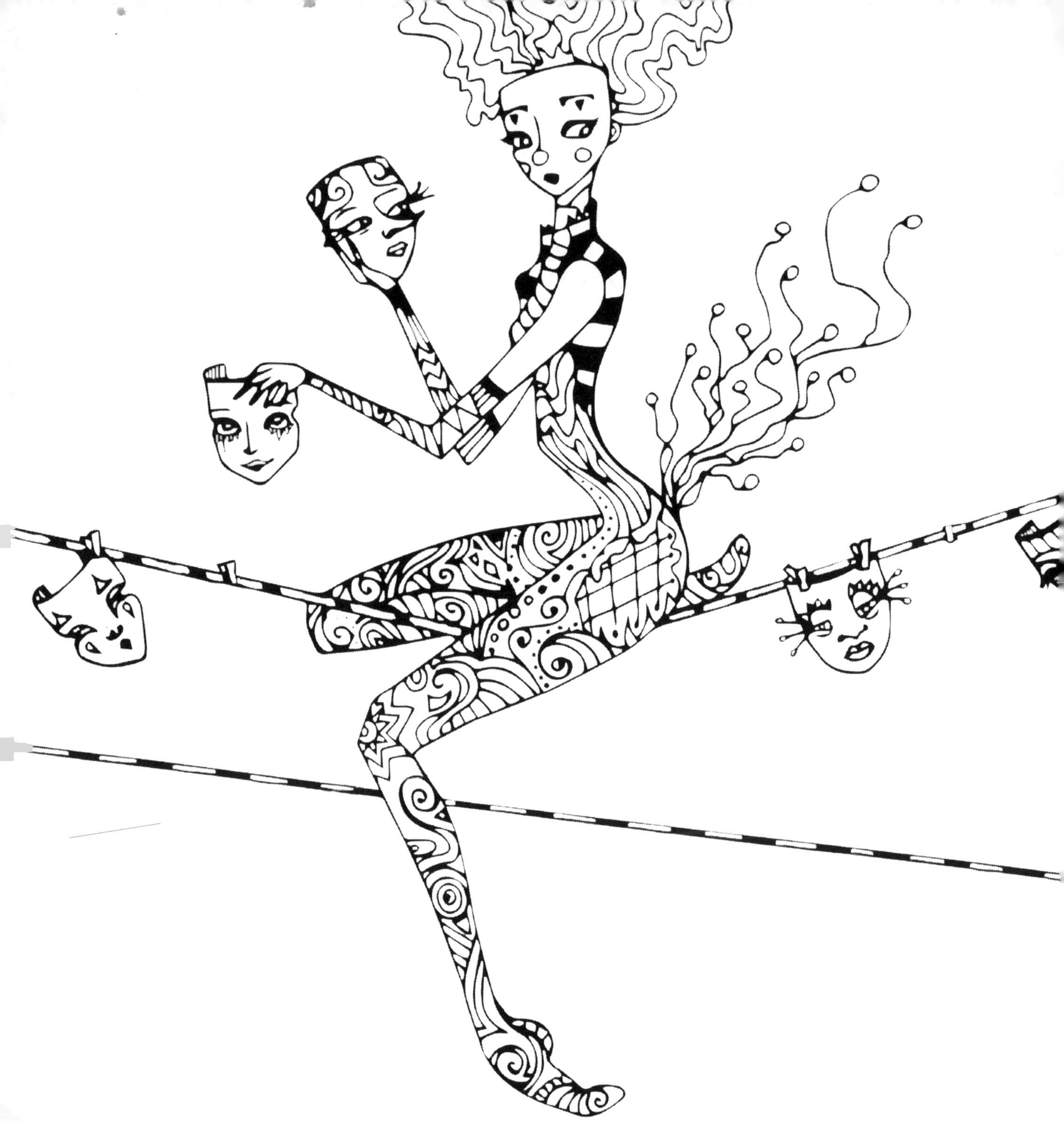

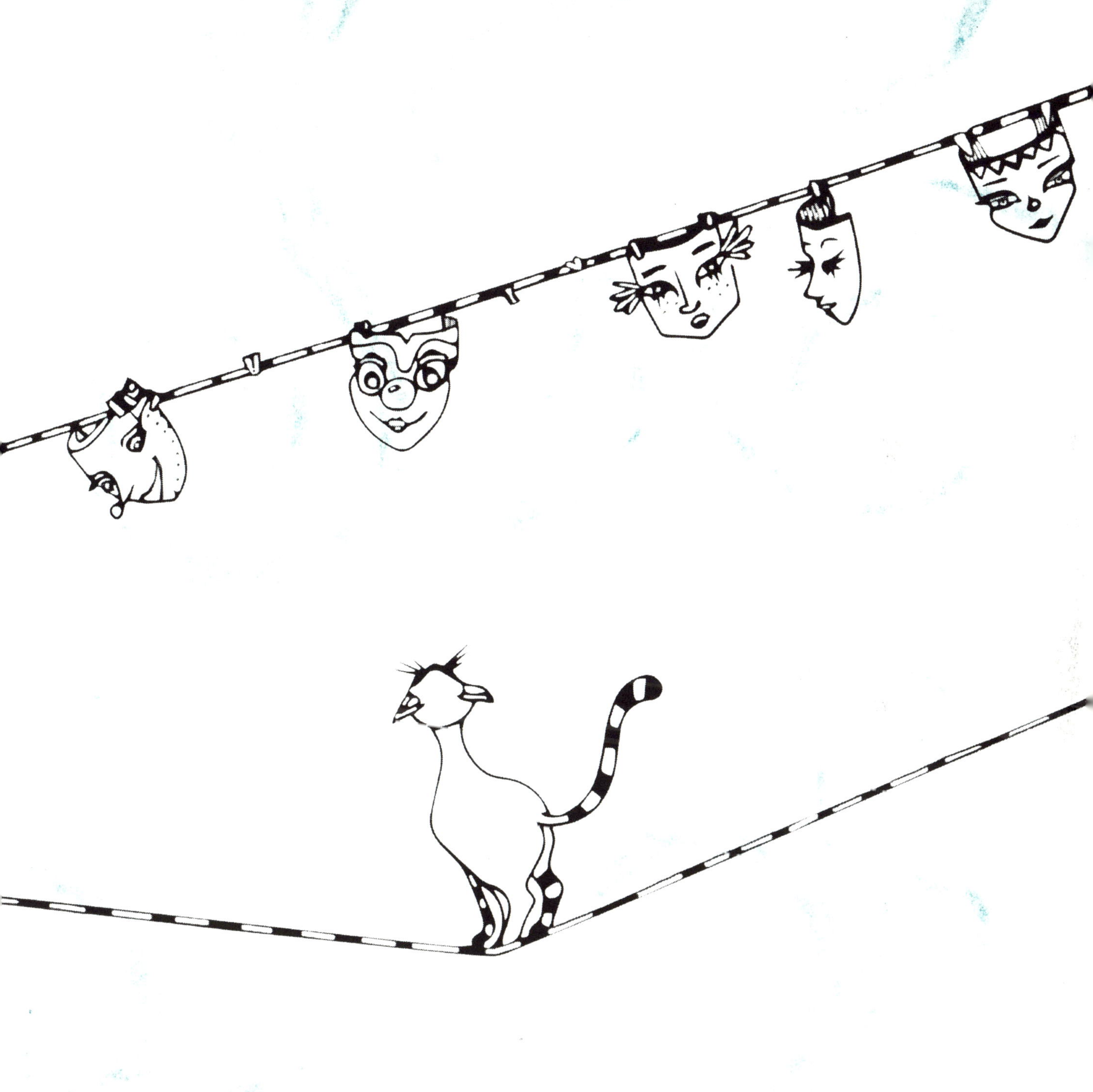

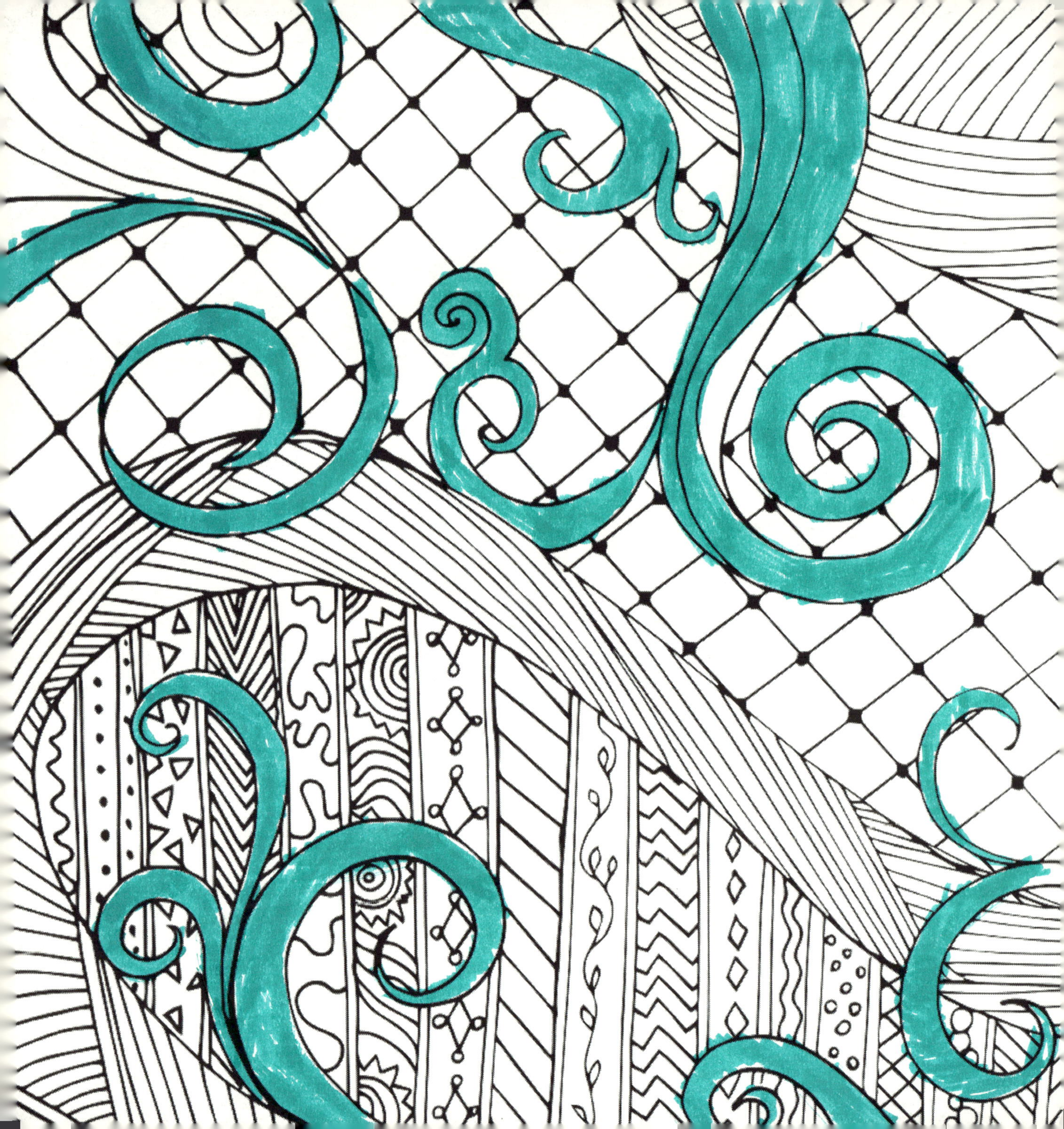

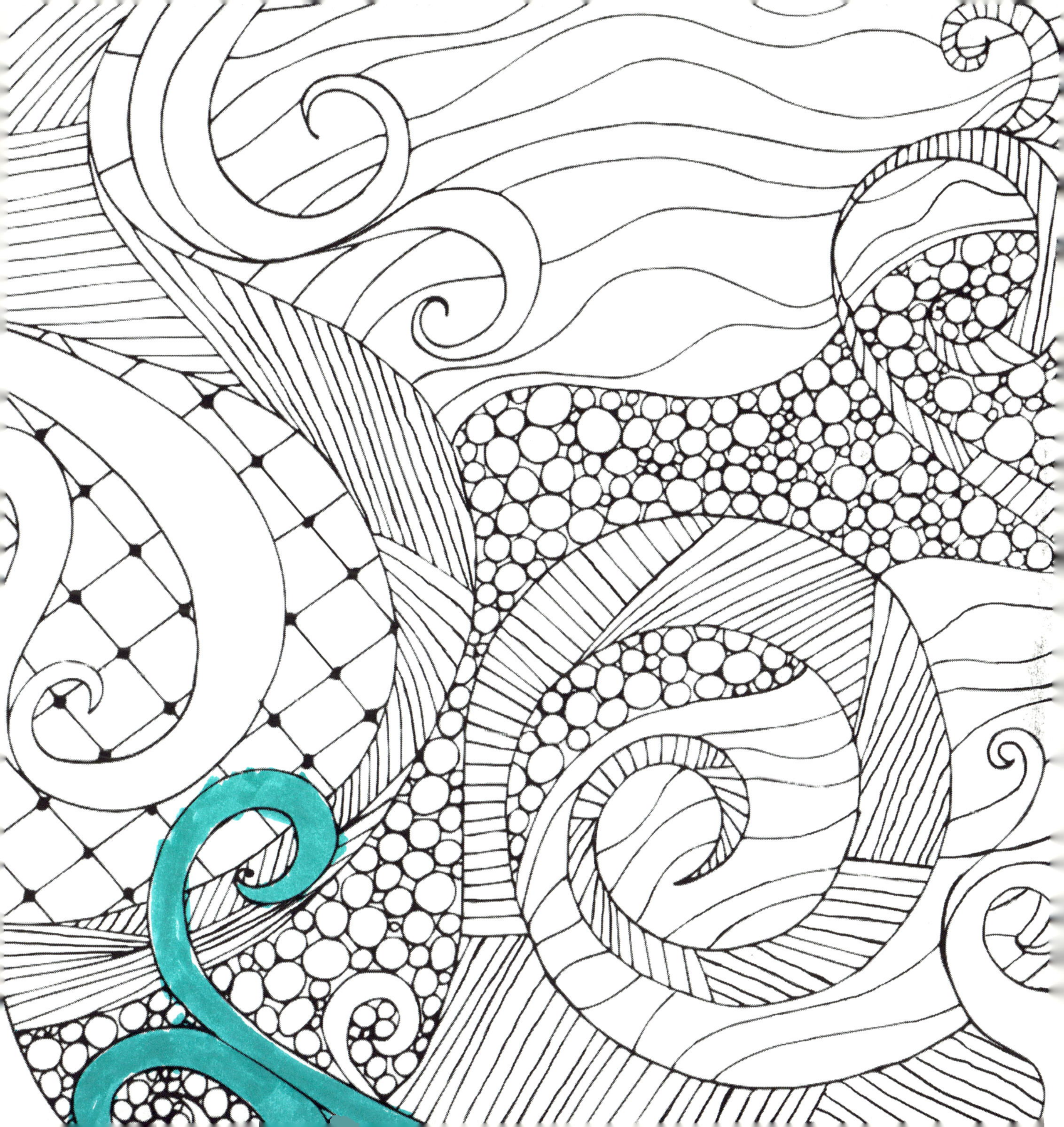

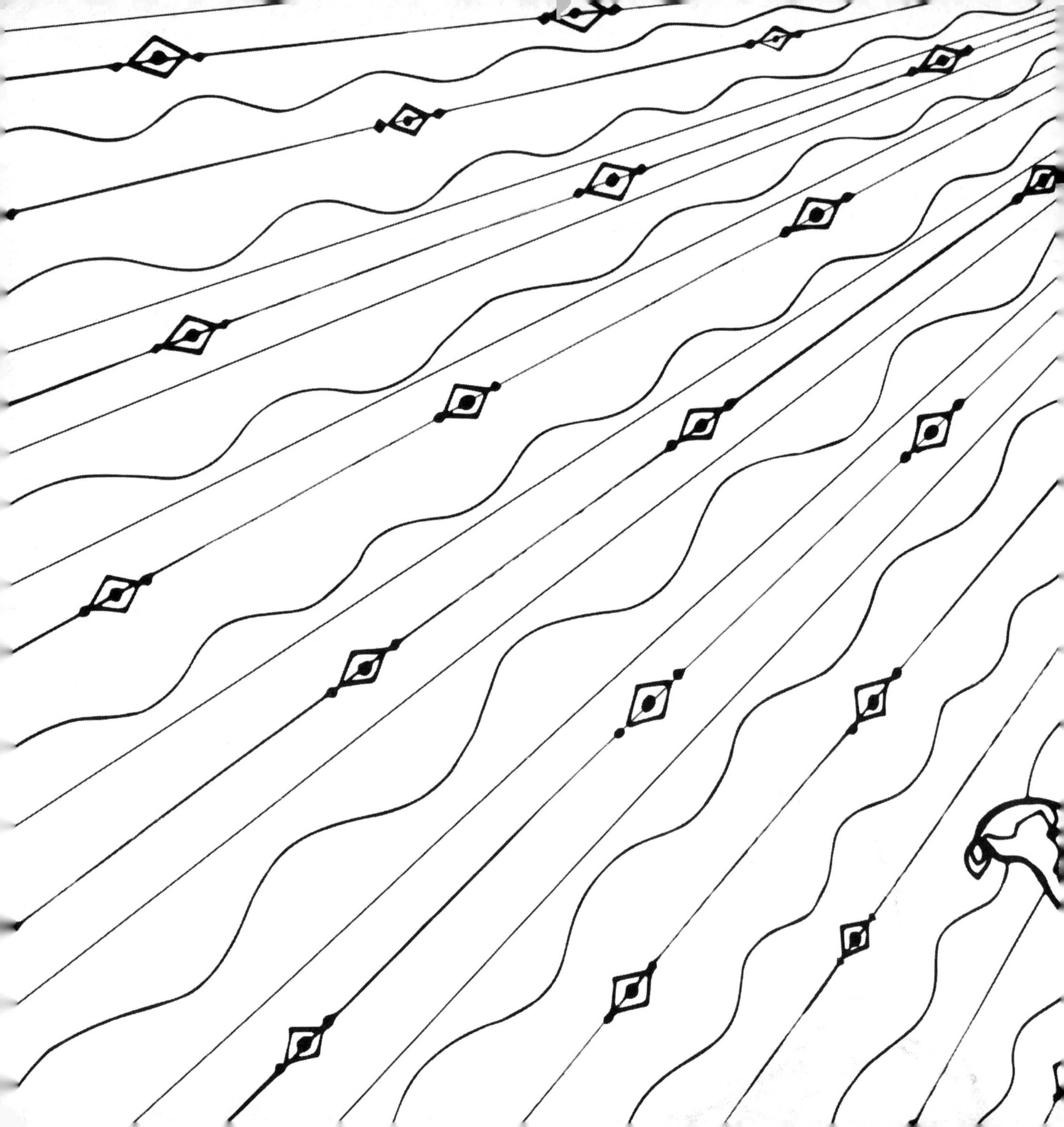

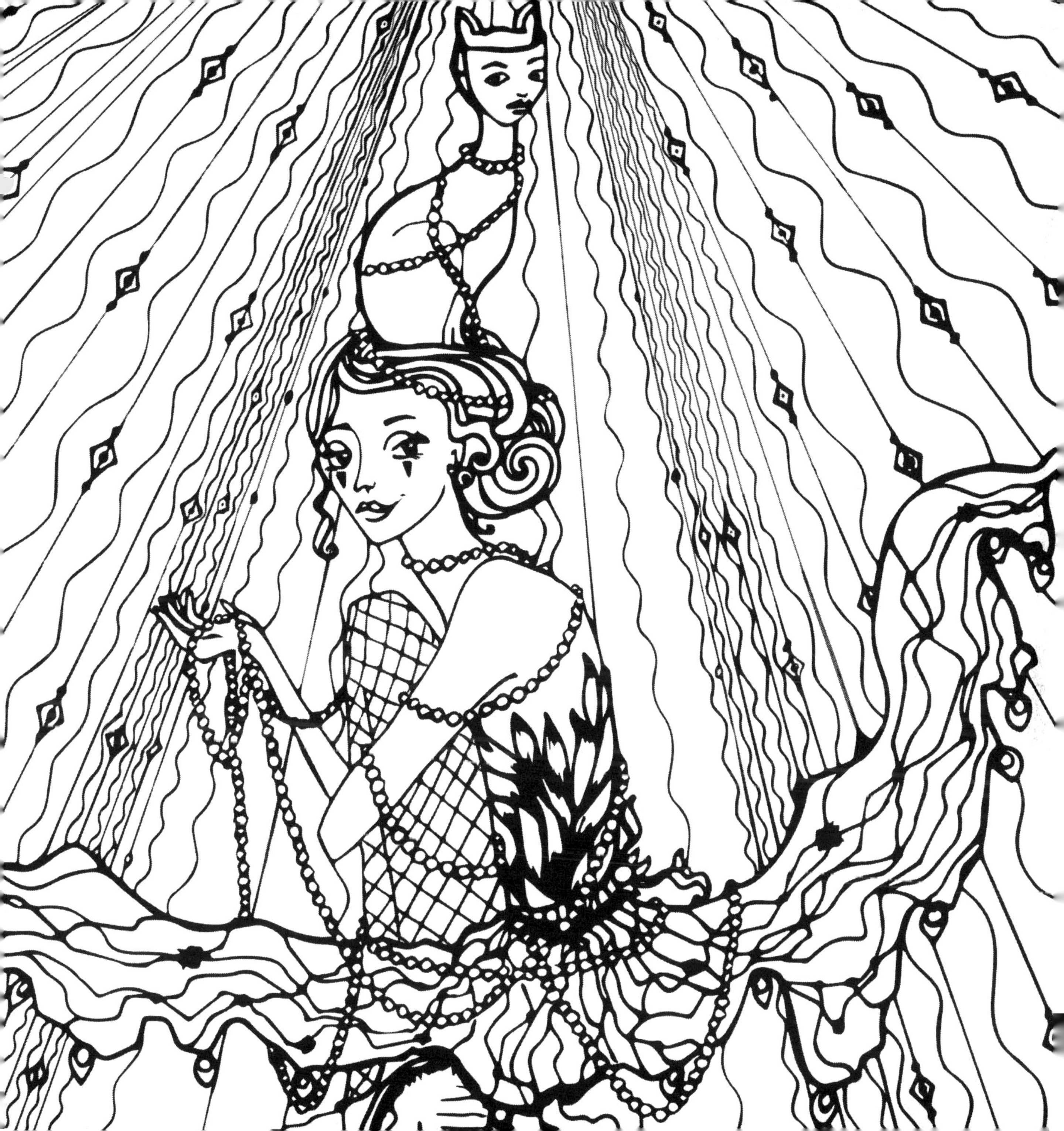

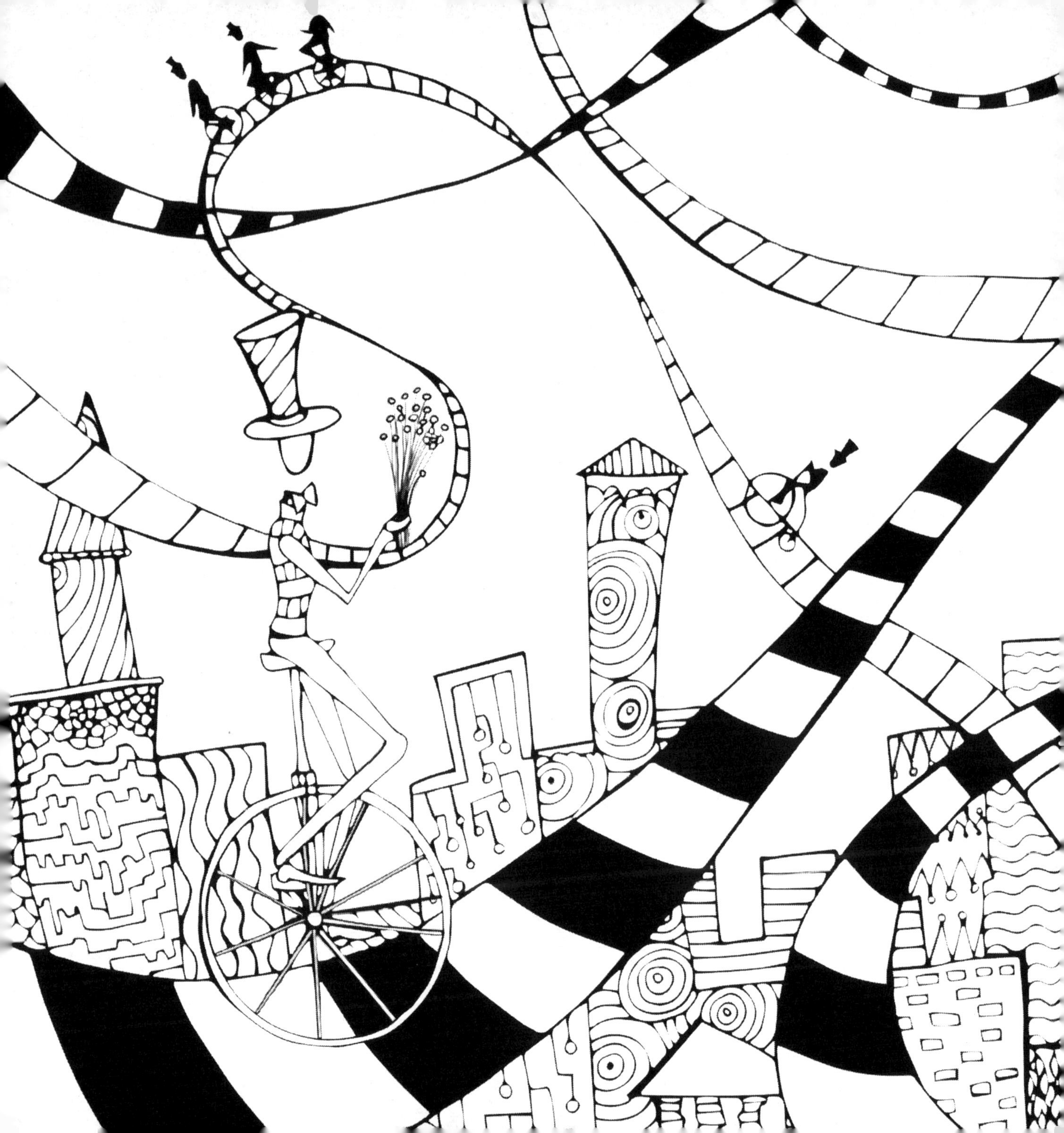

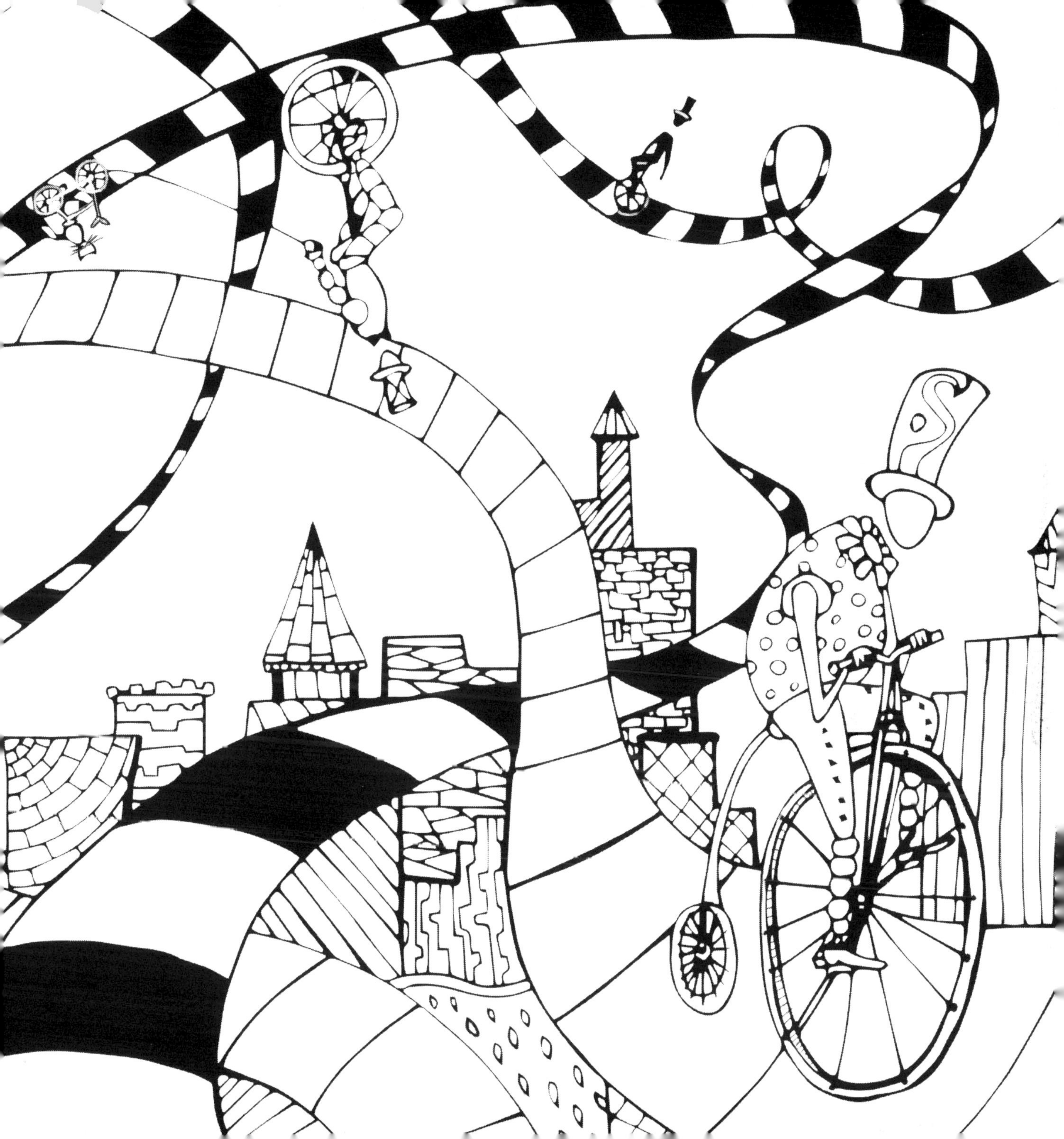

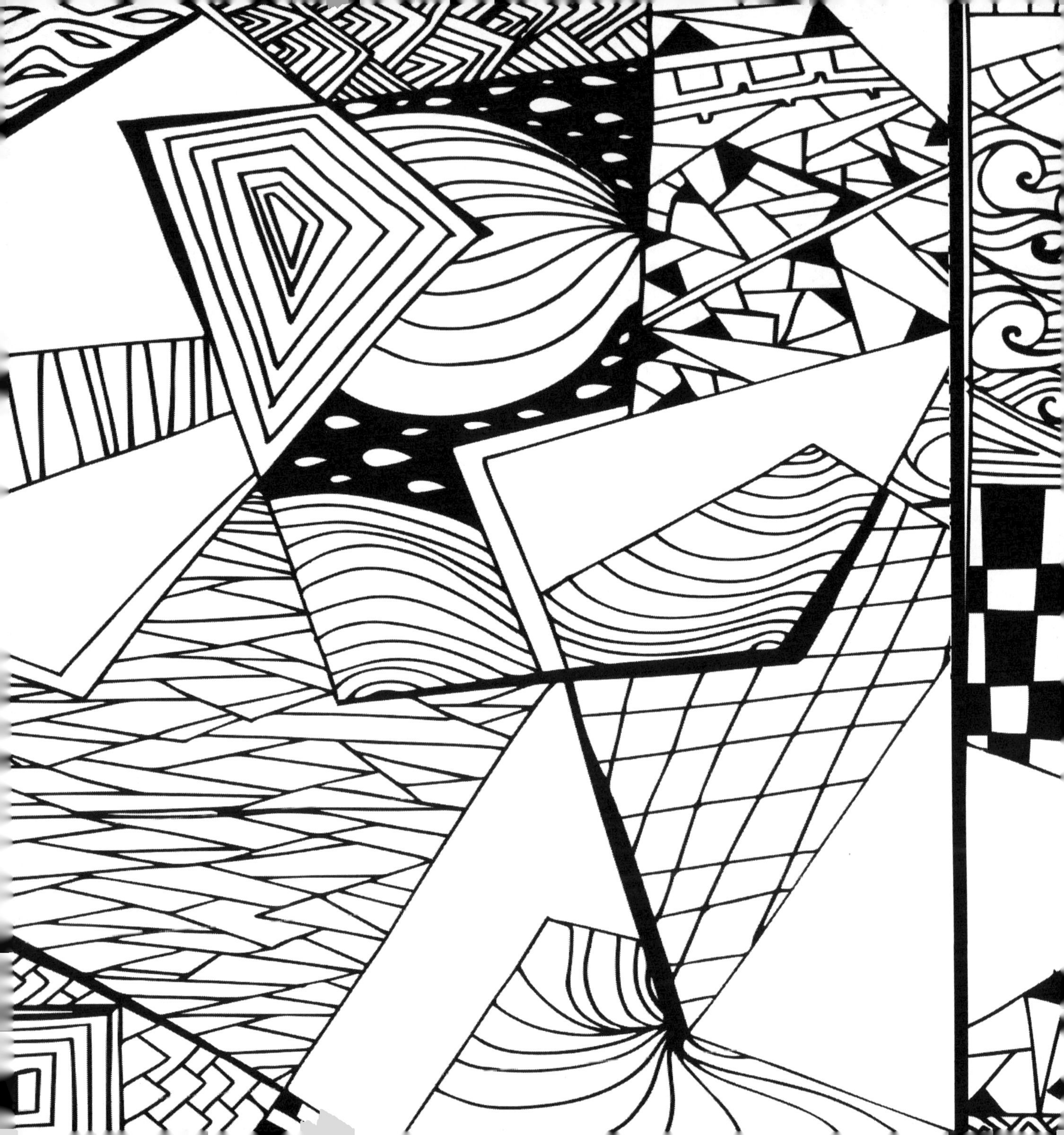

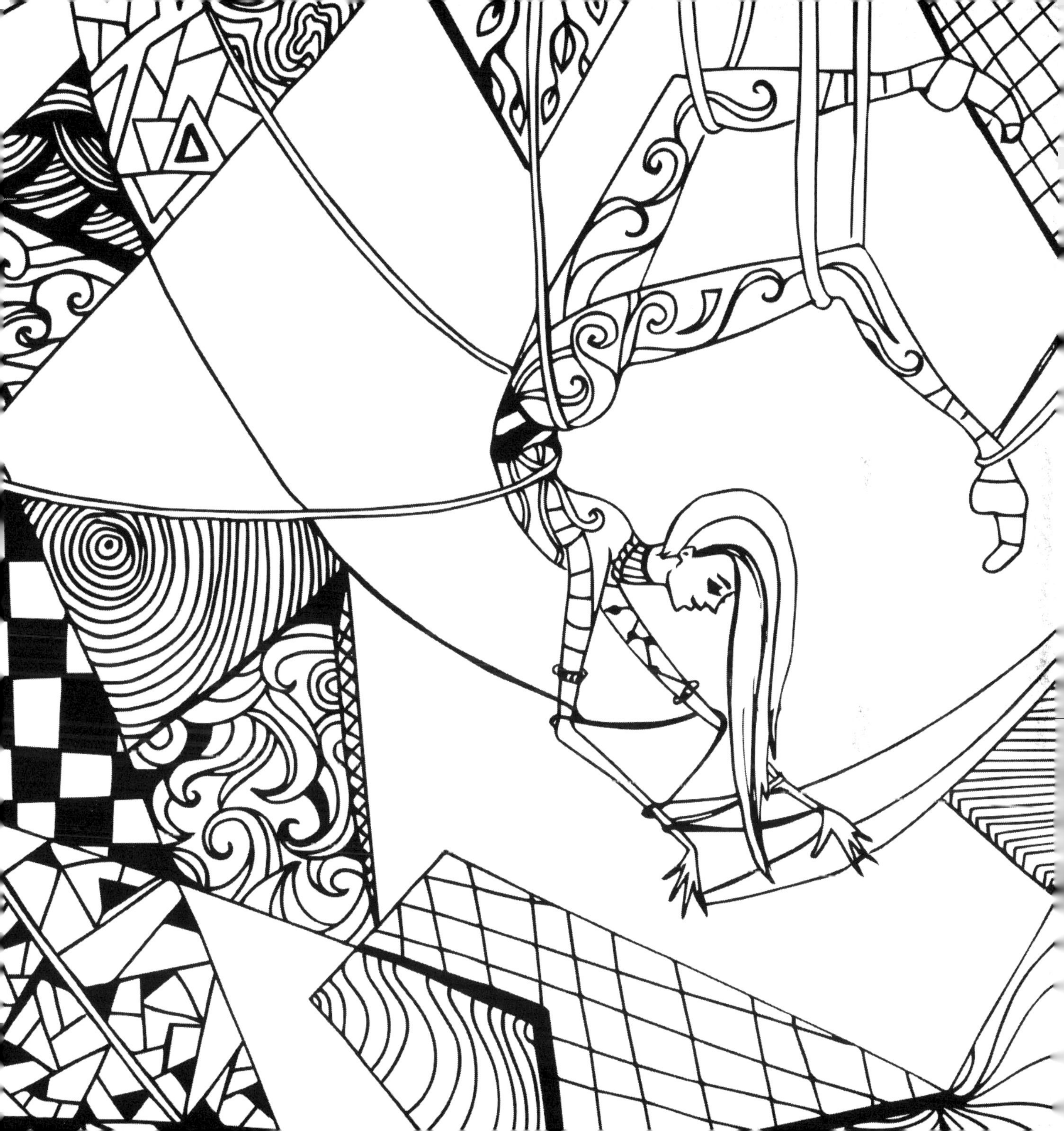

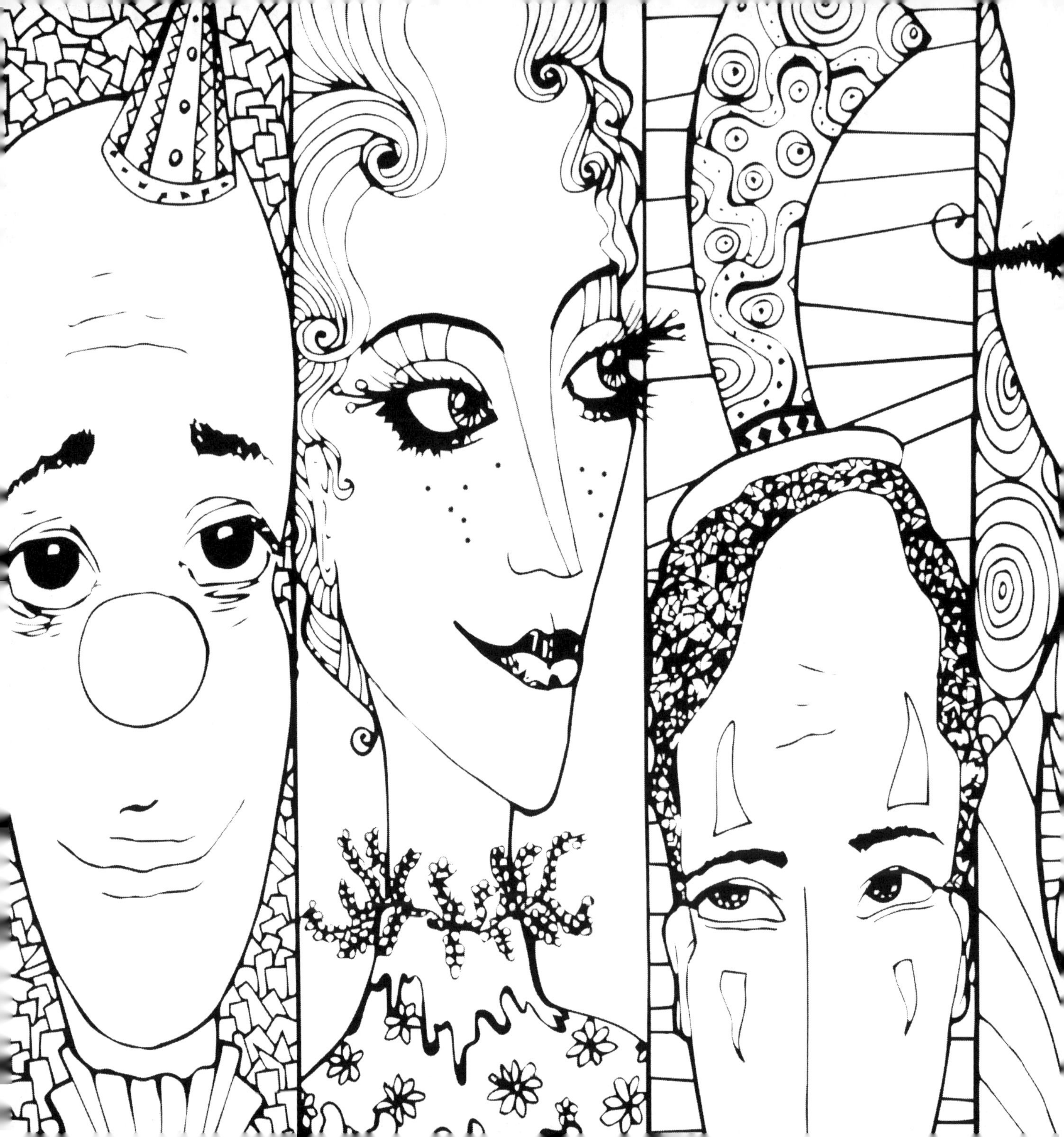

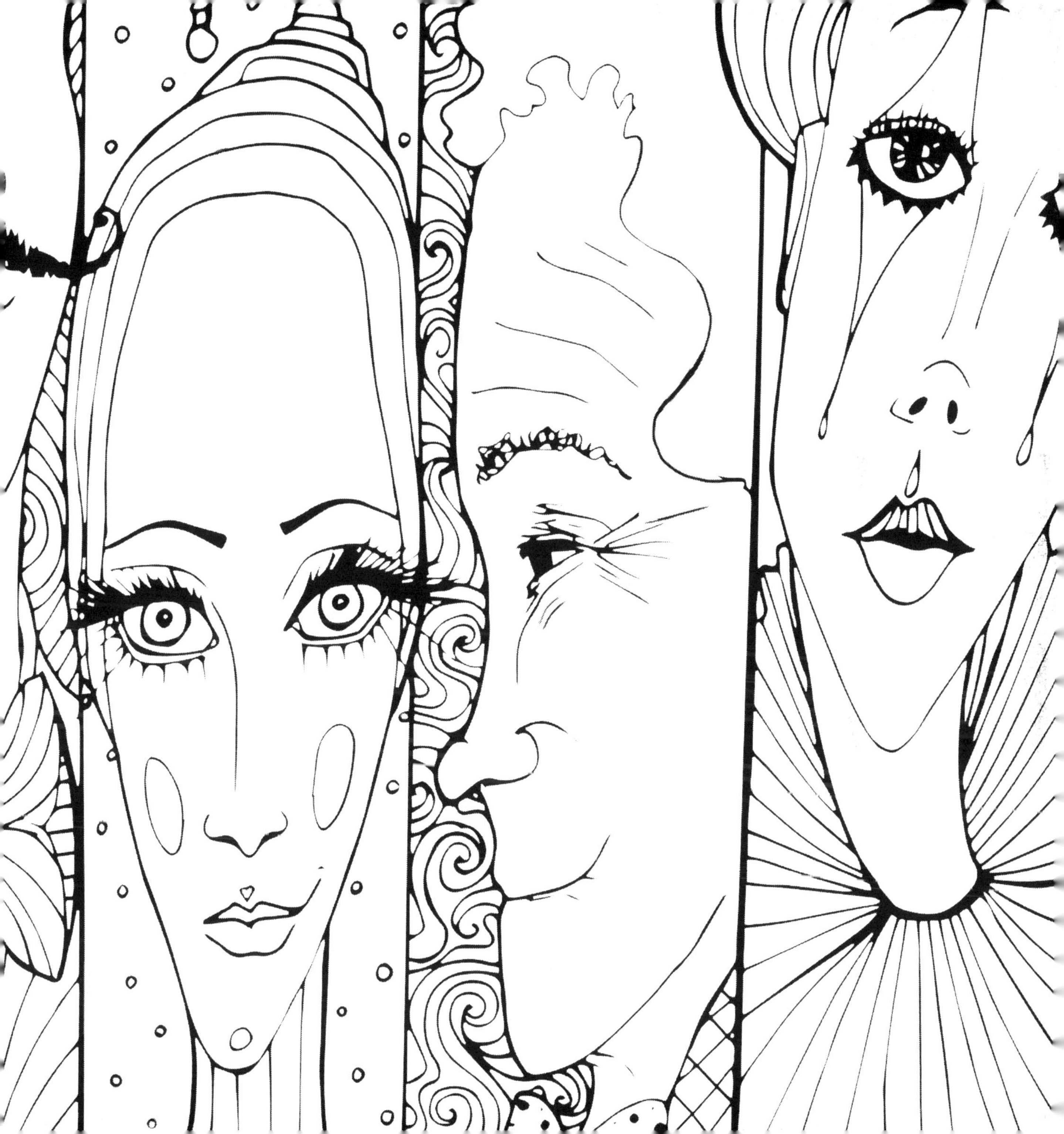

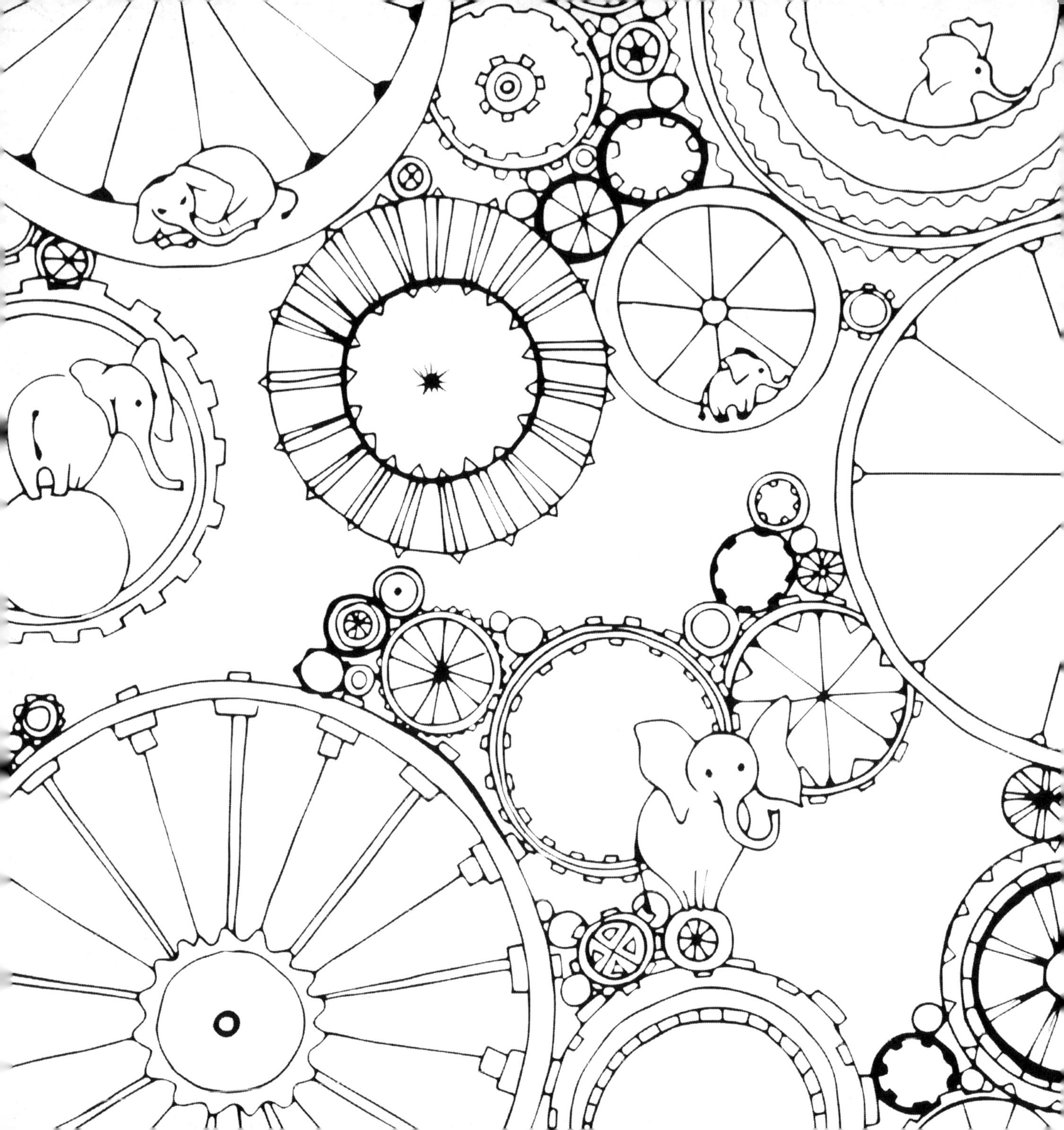

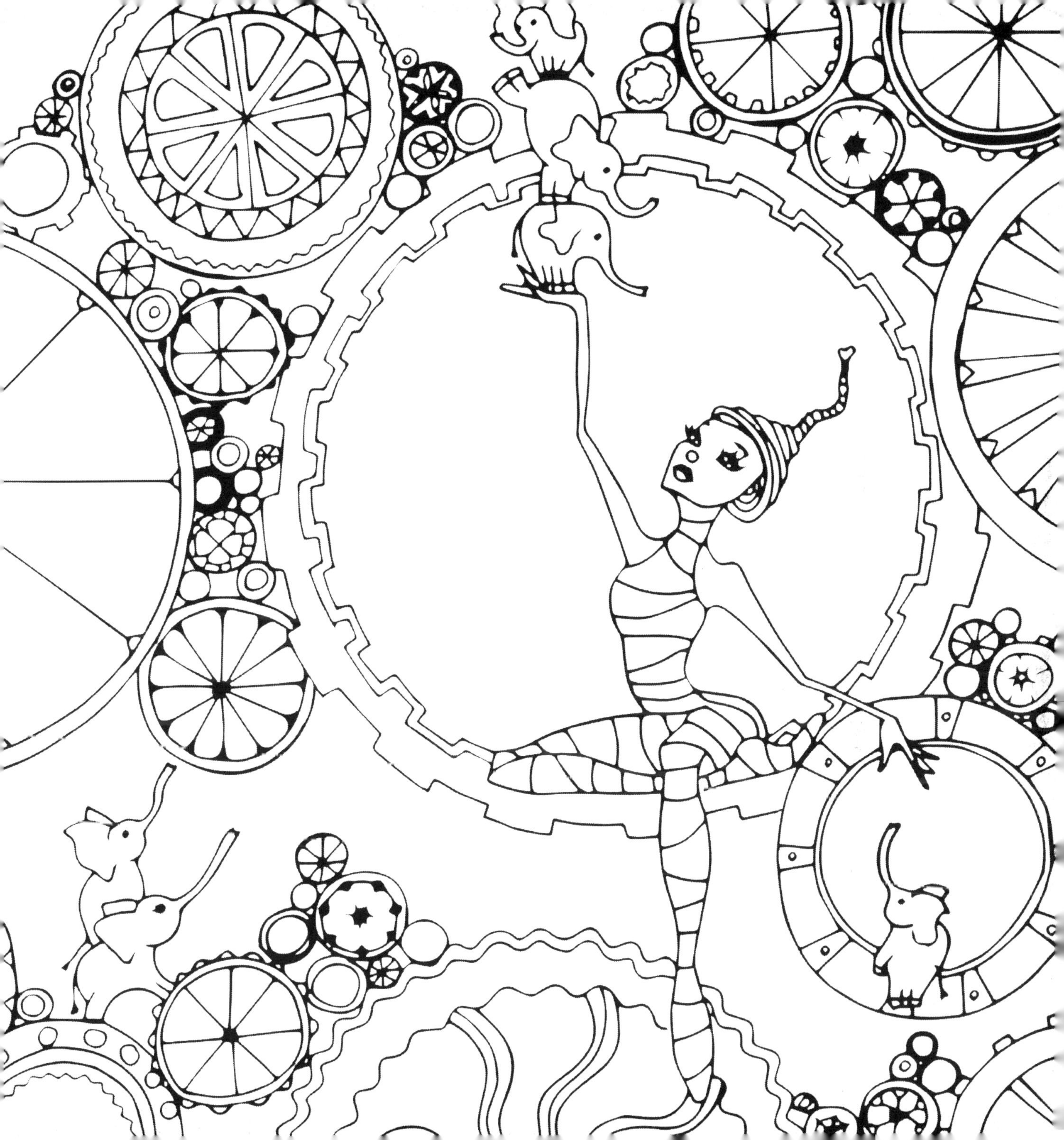

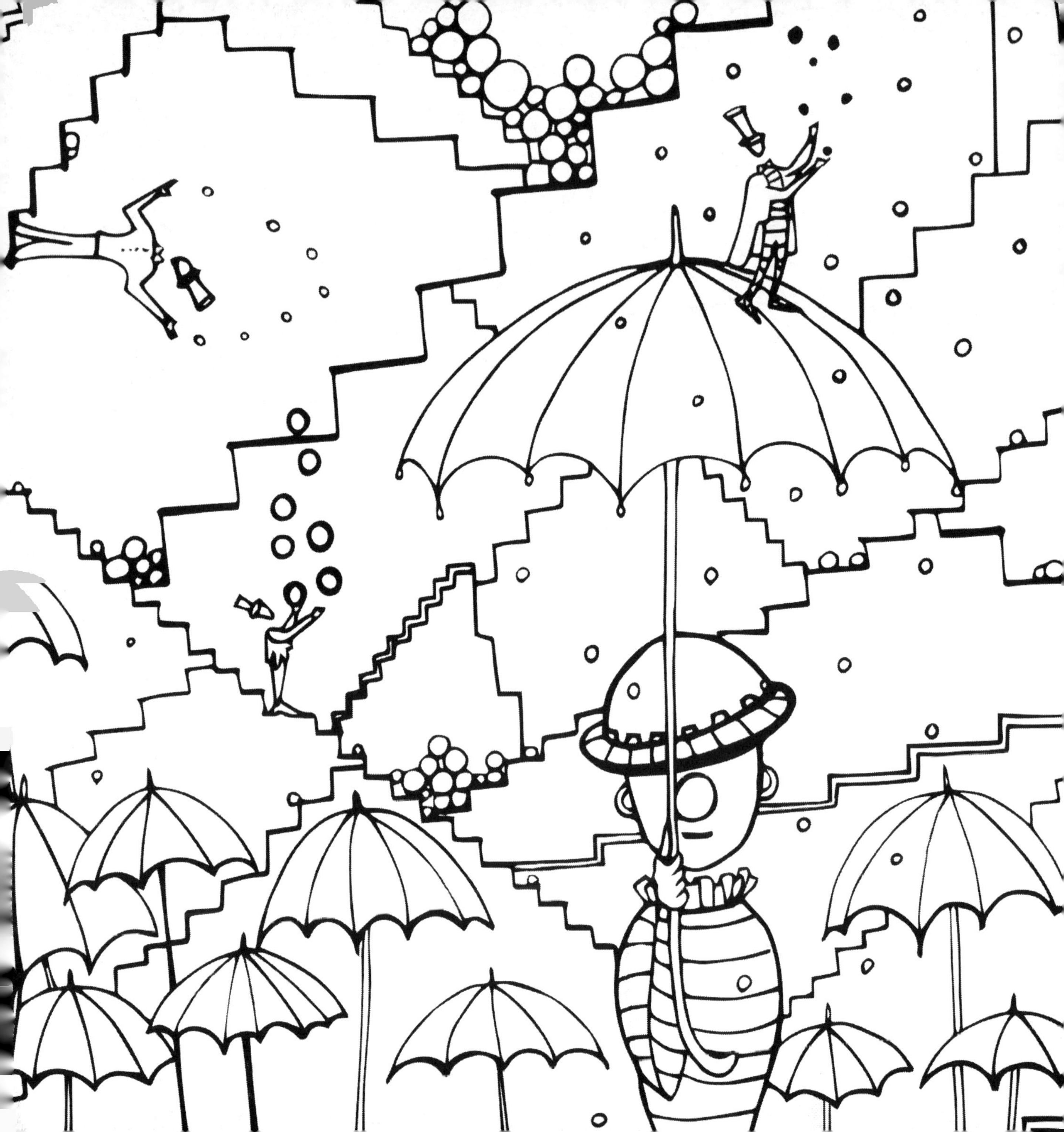

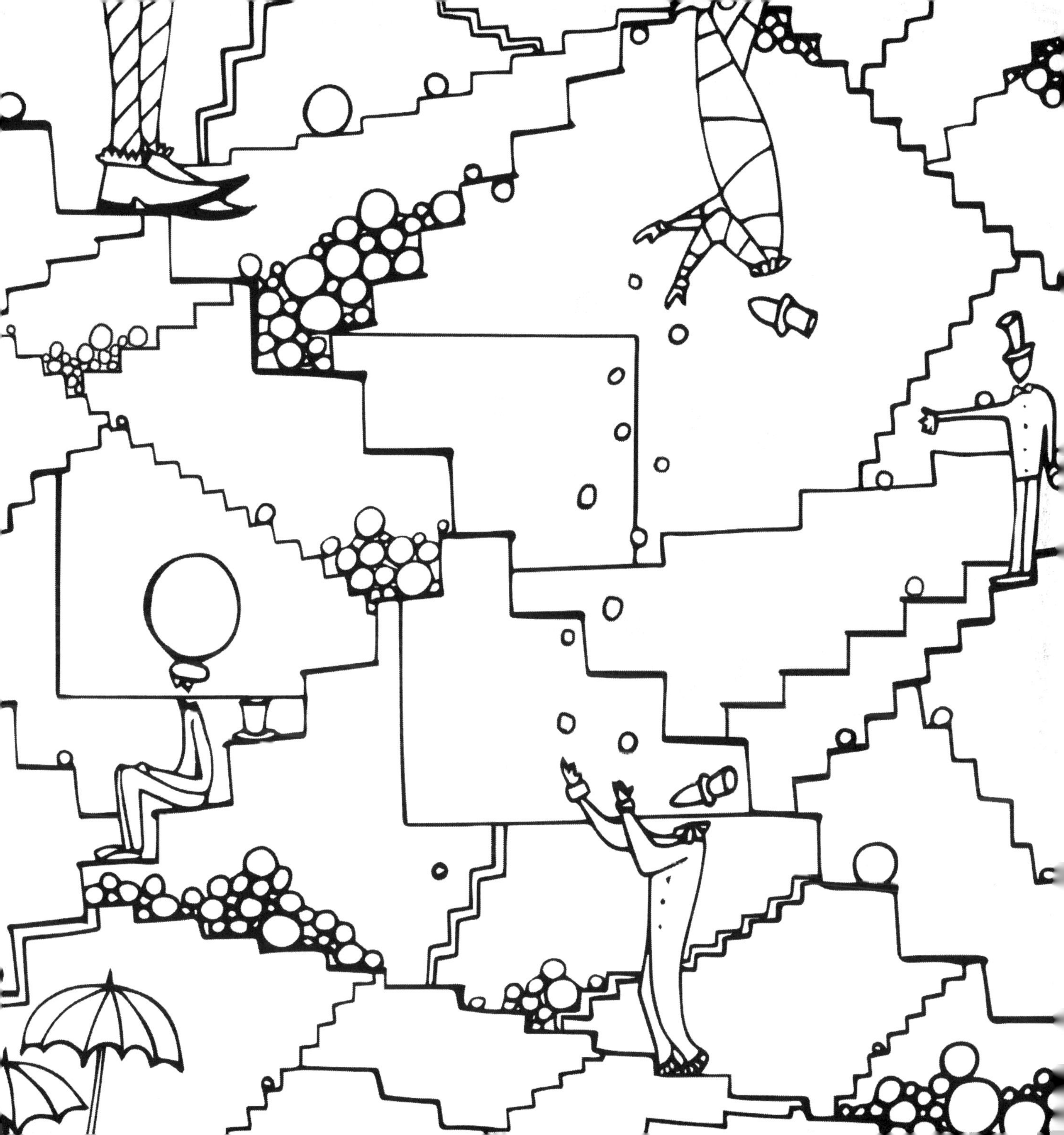

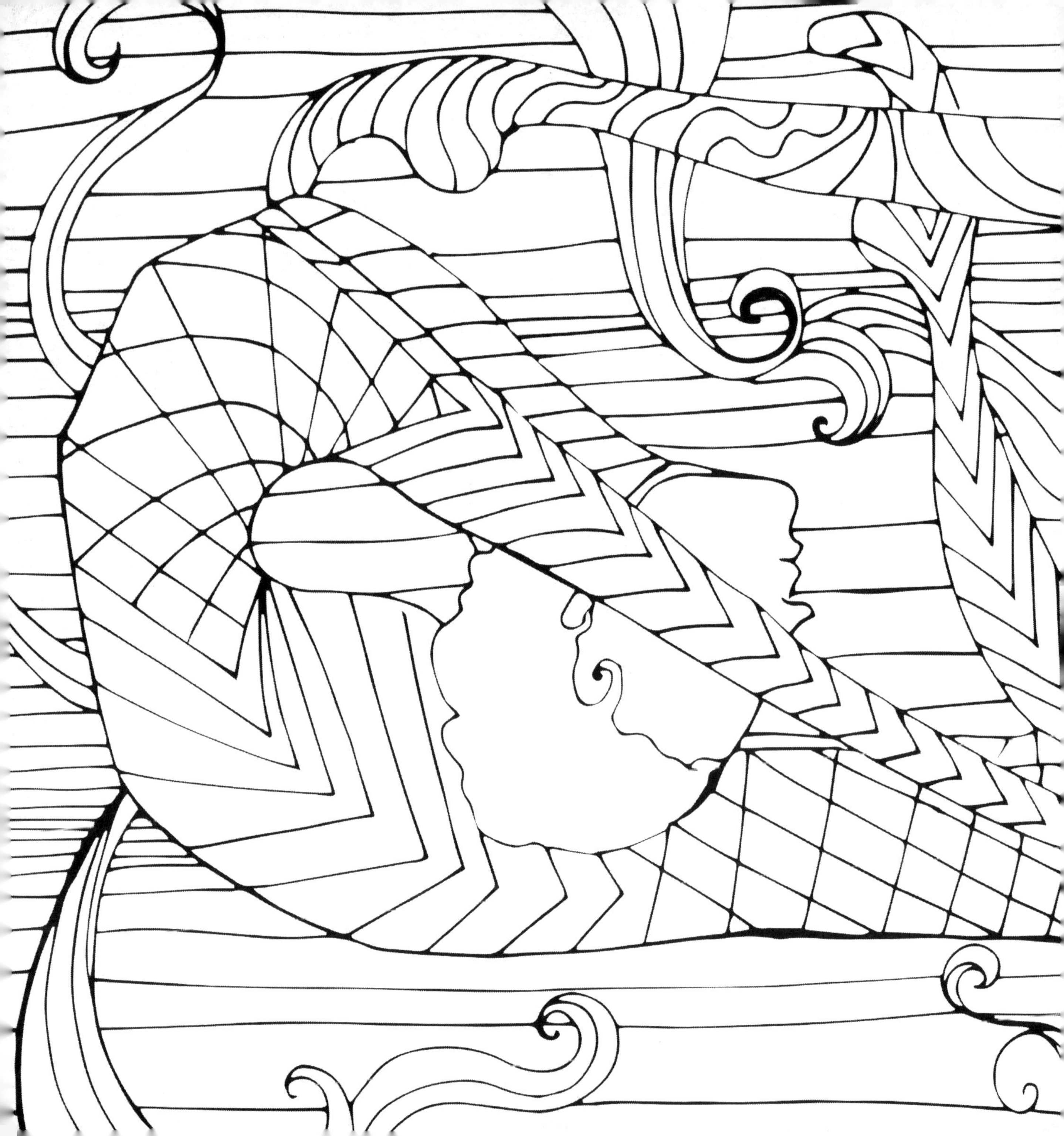

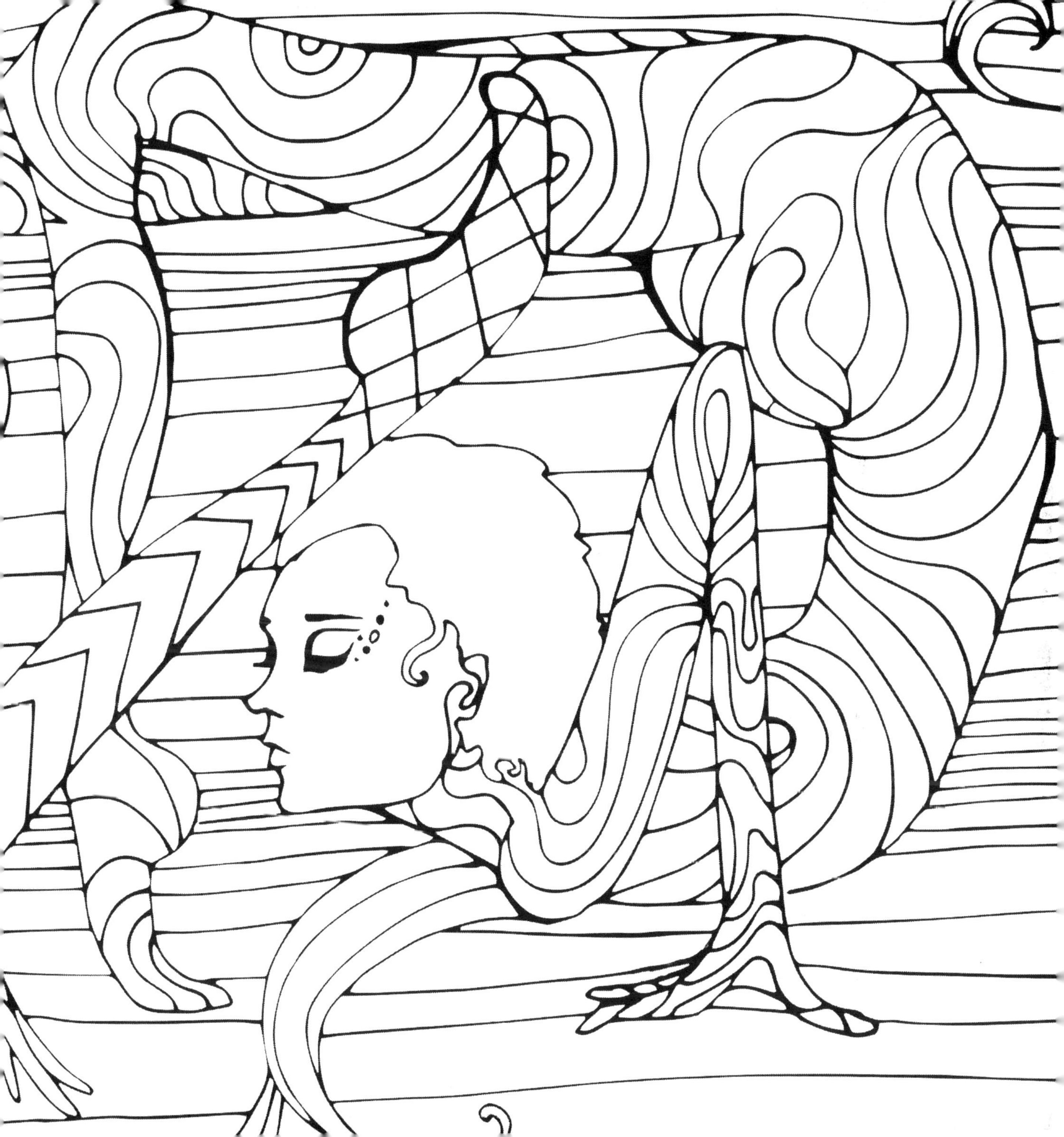

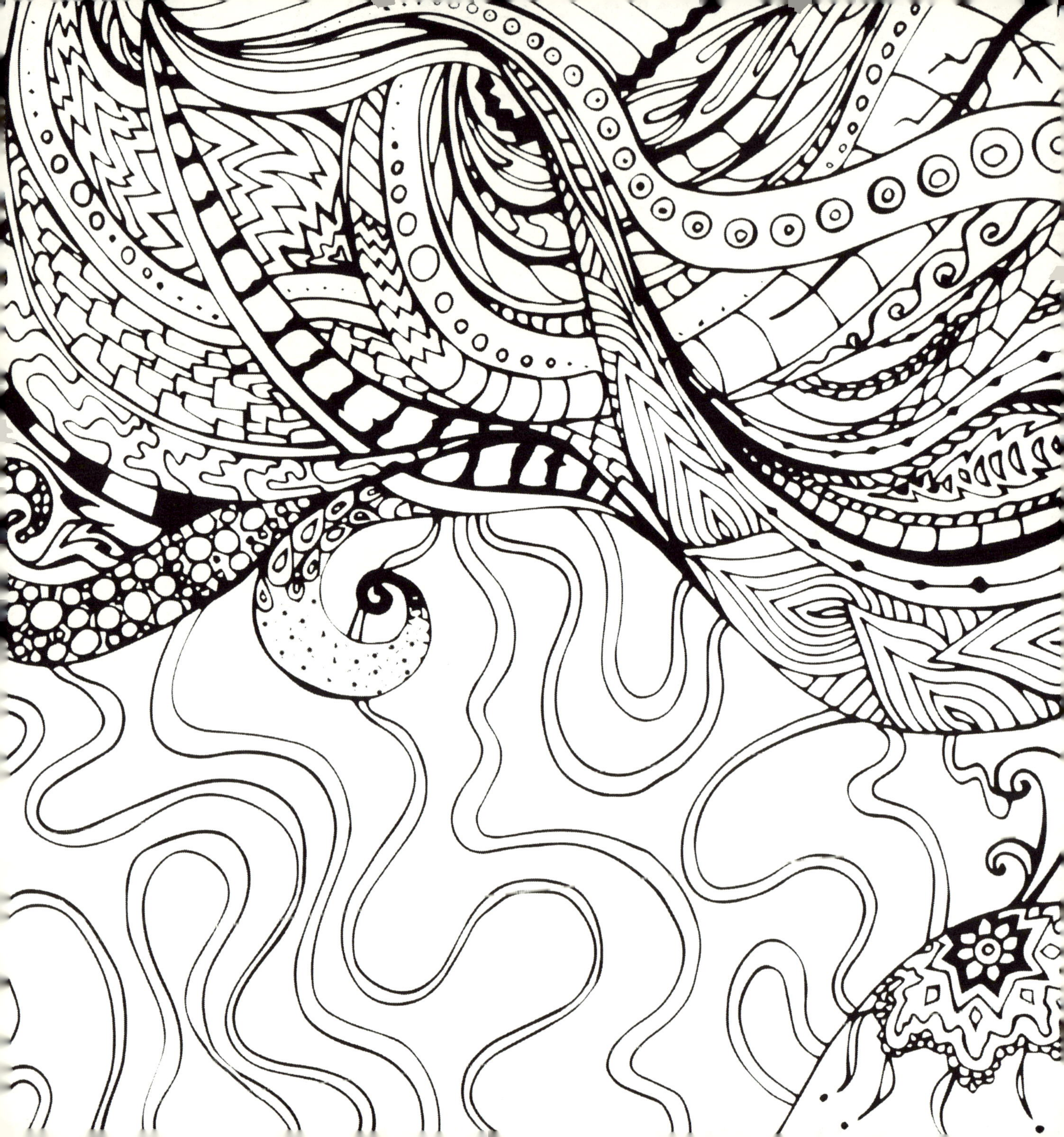

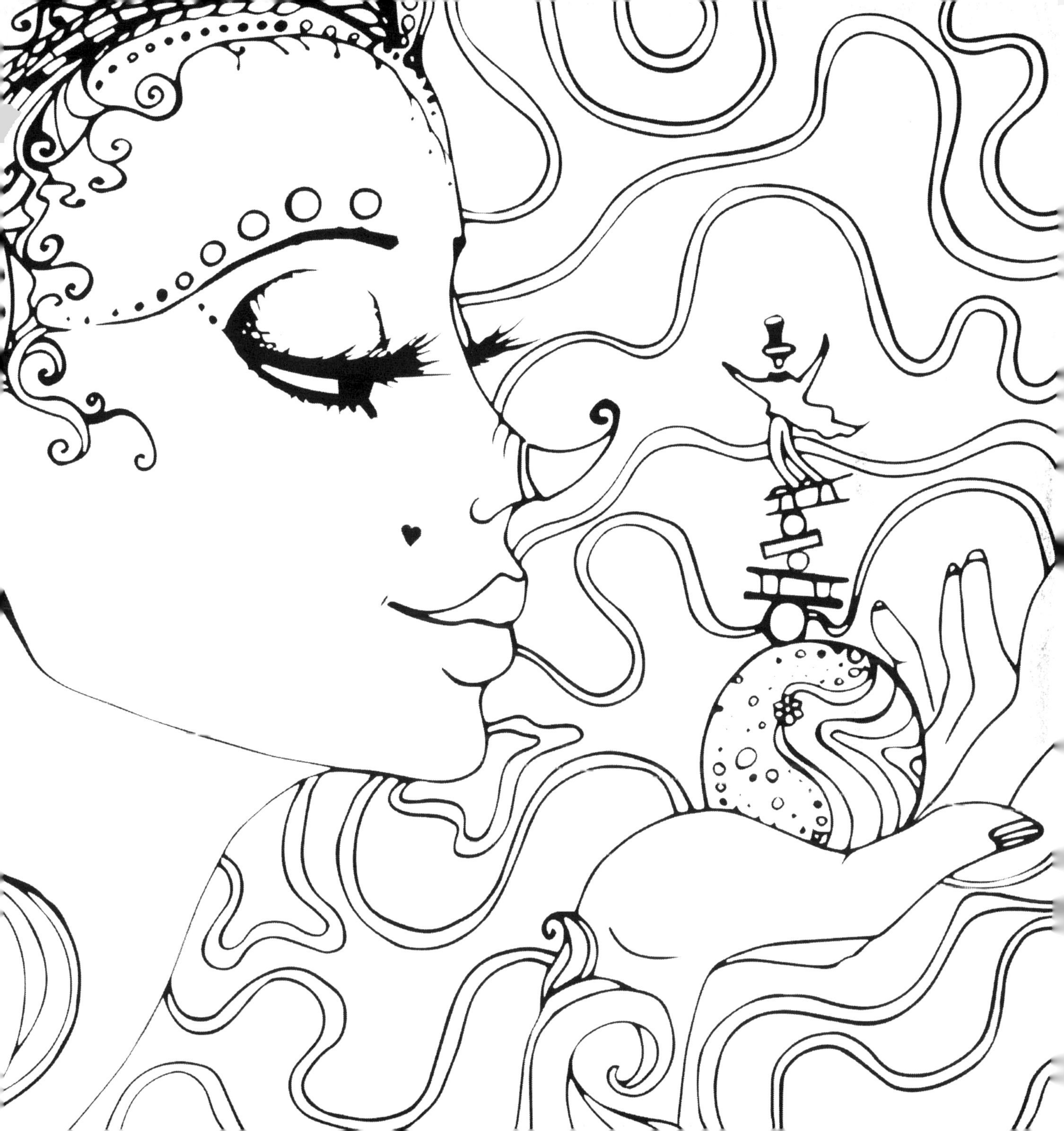

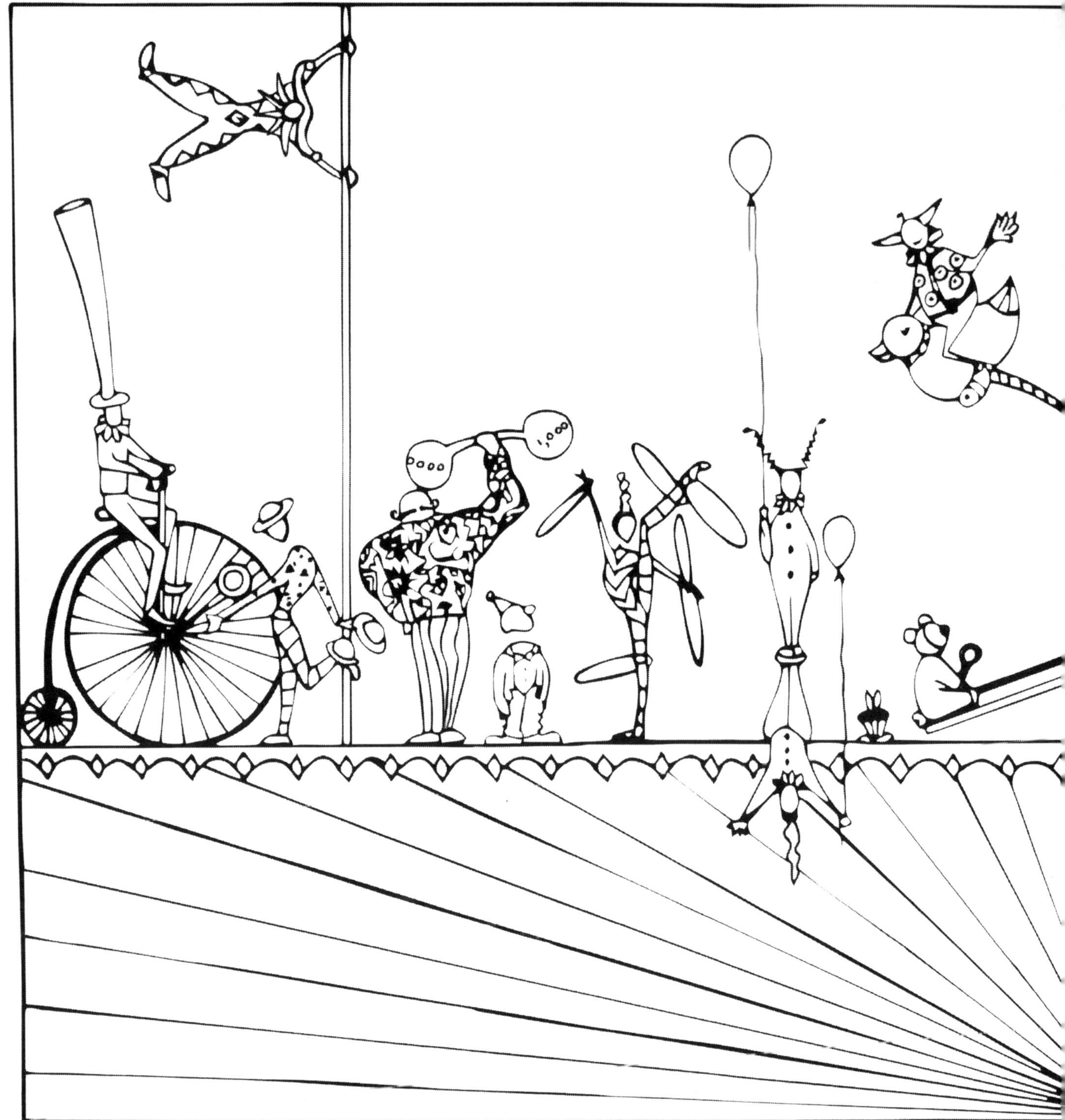
0000
1,000

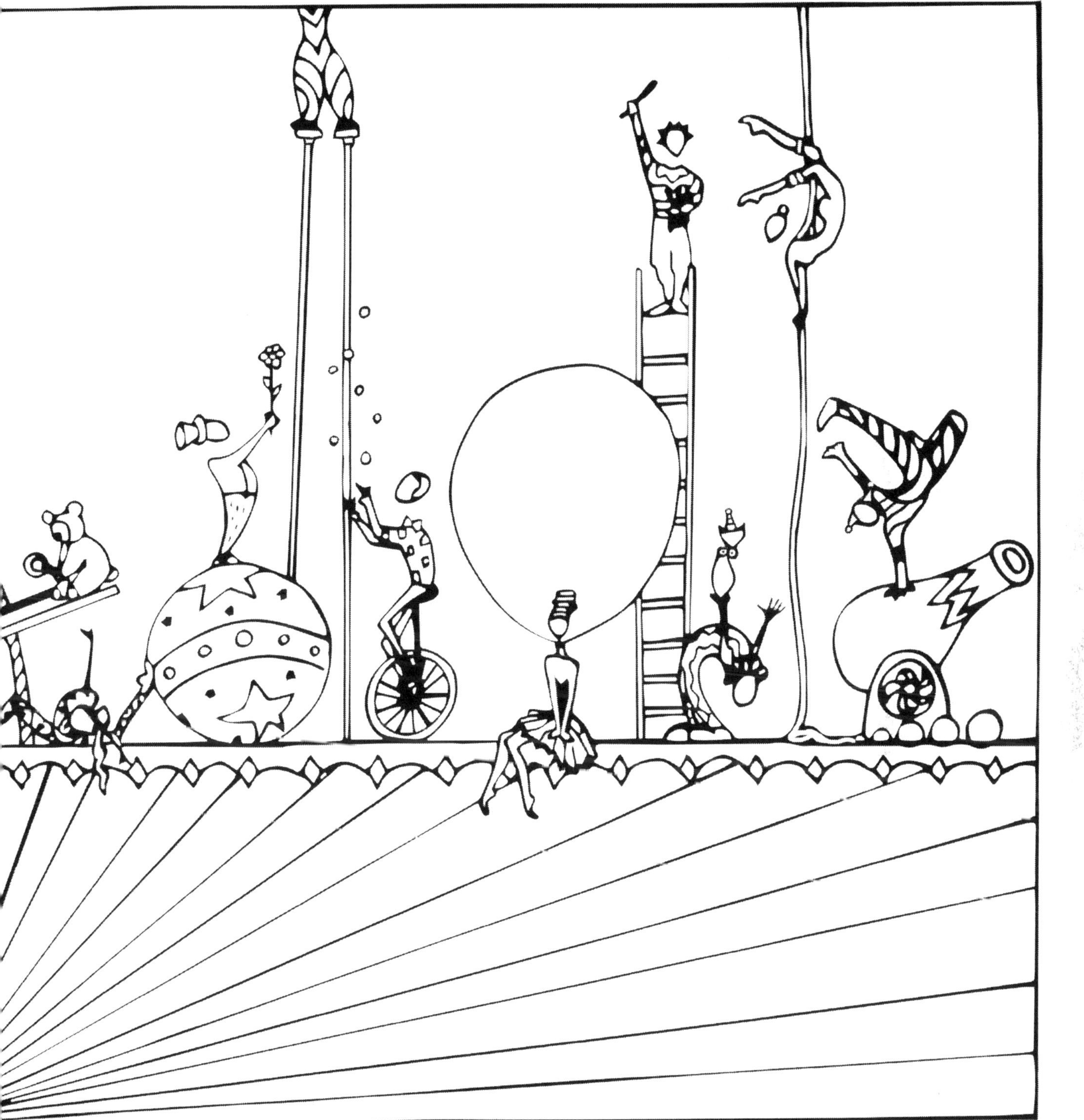

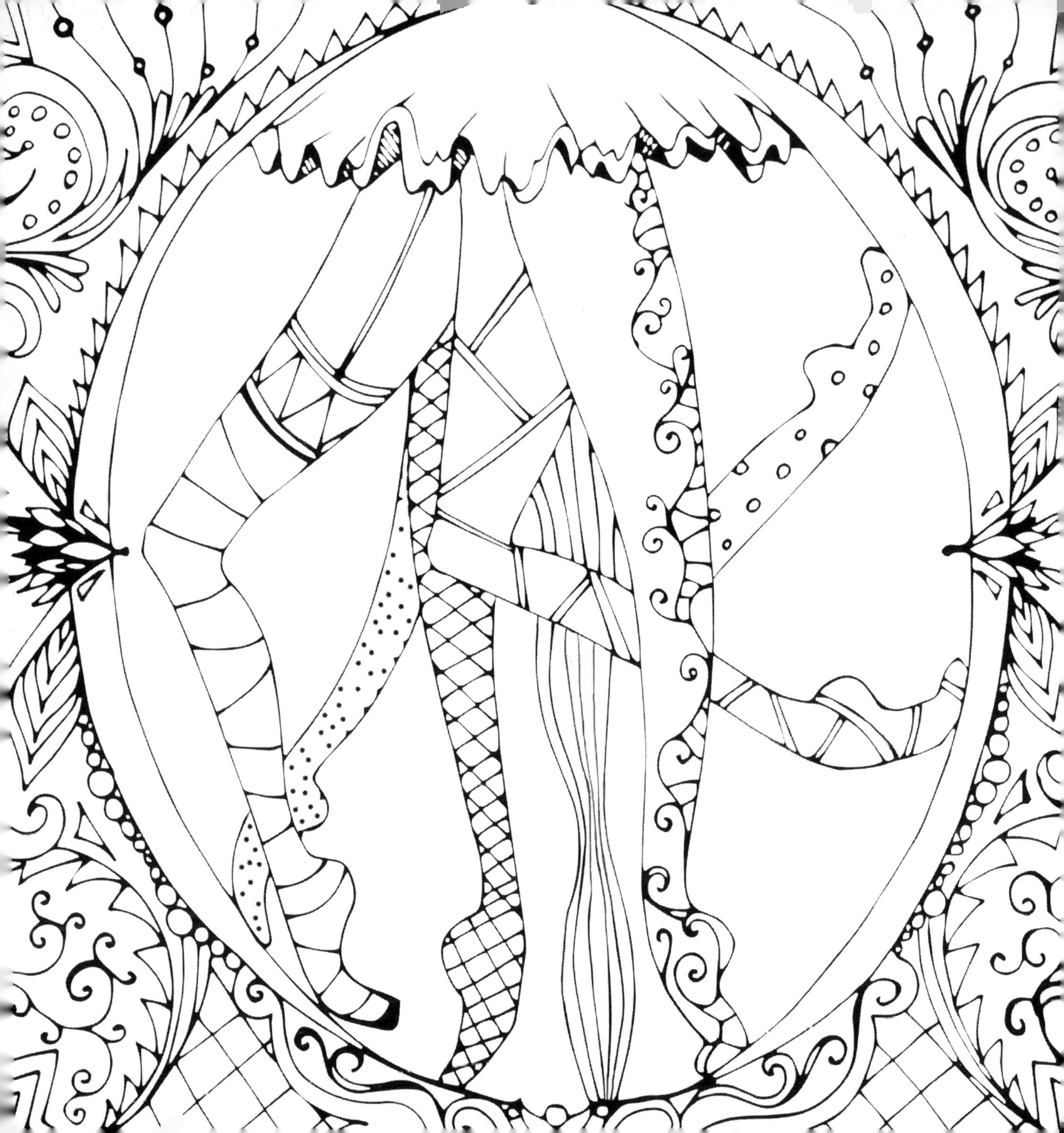

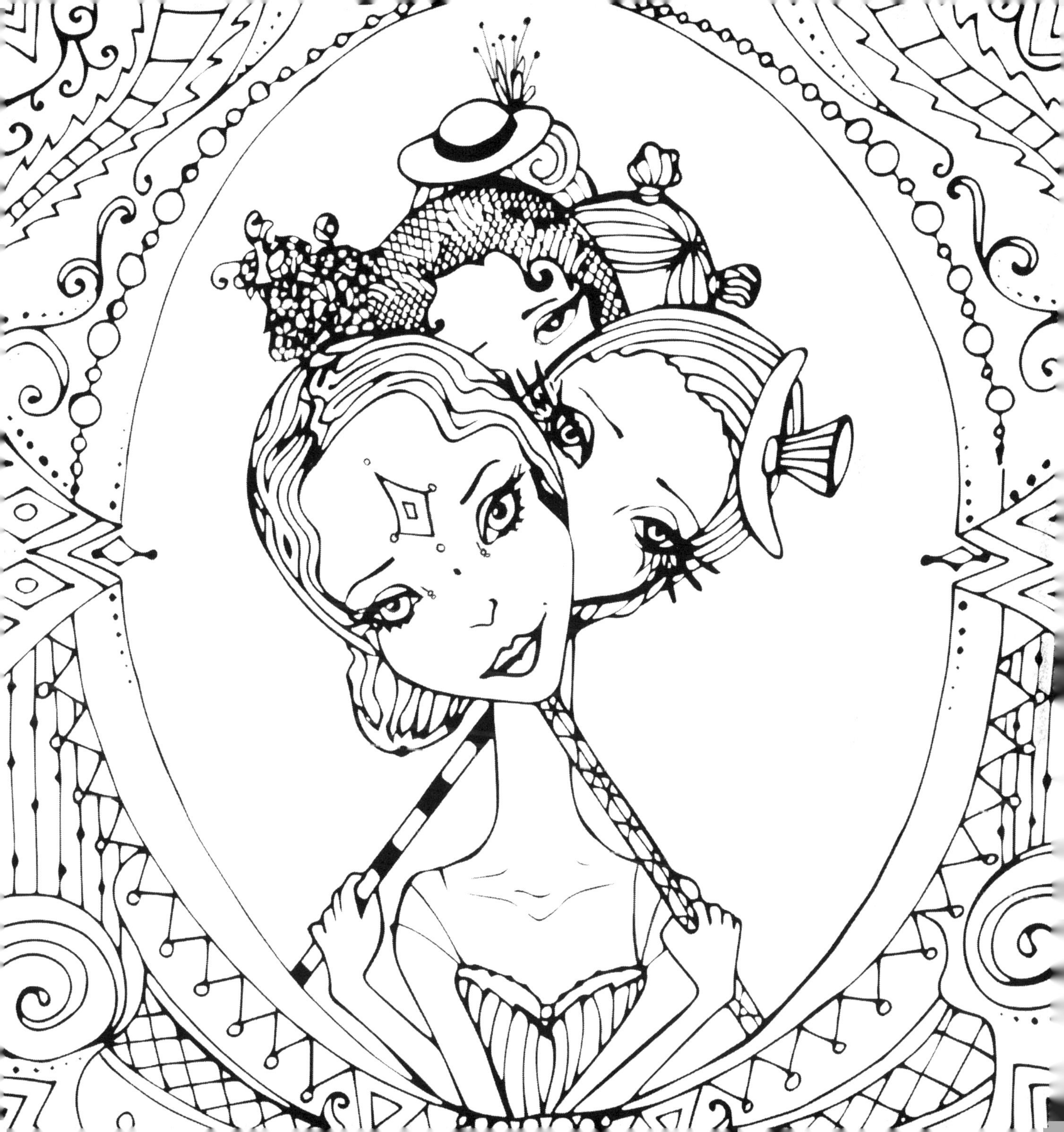

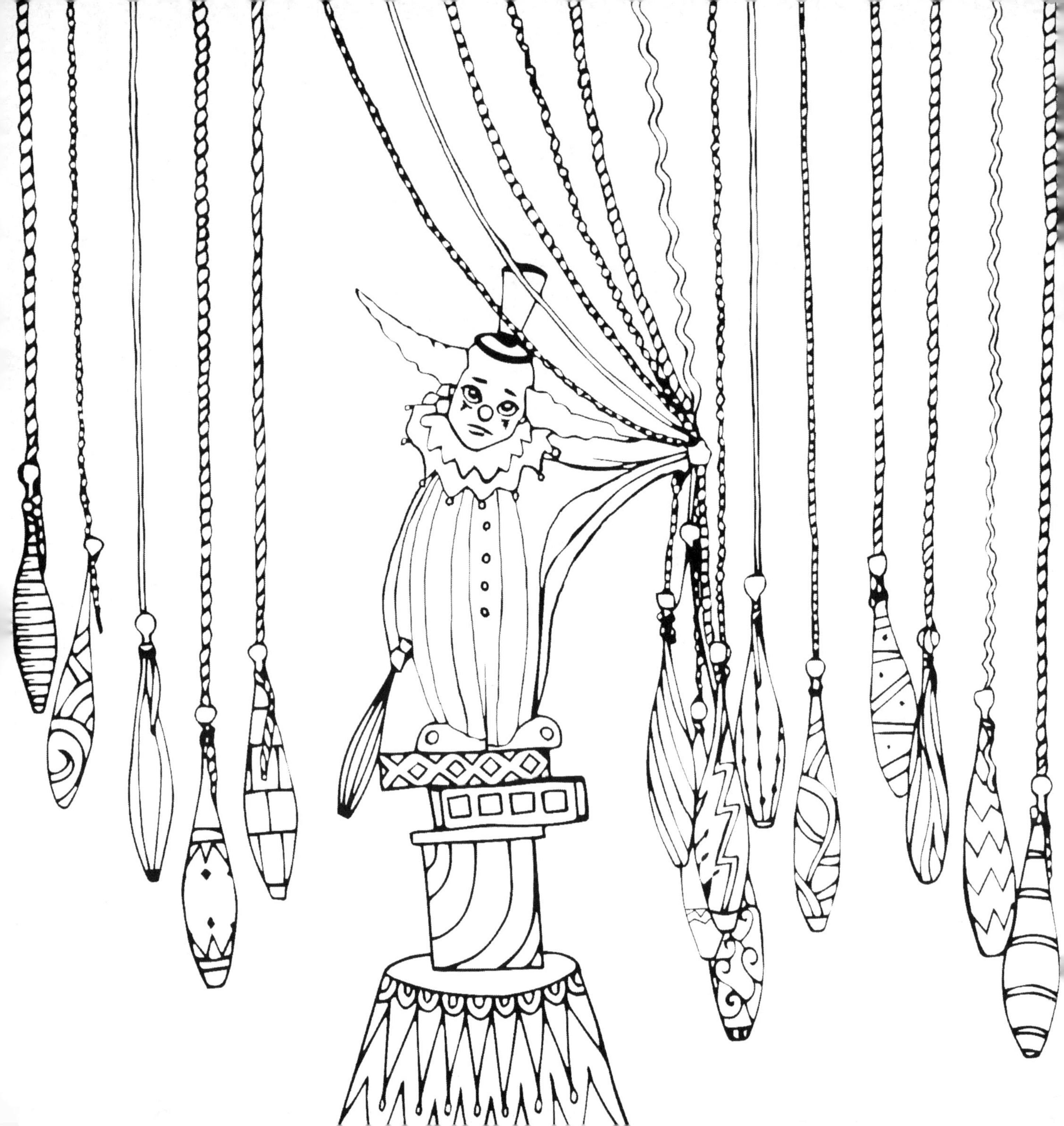

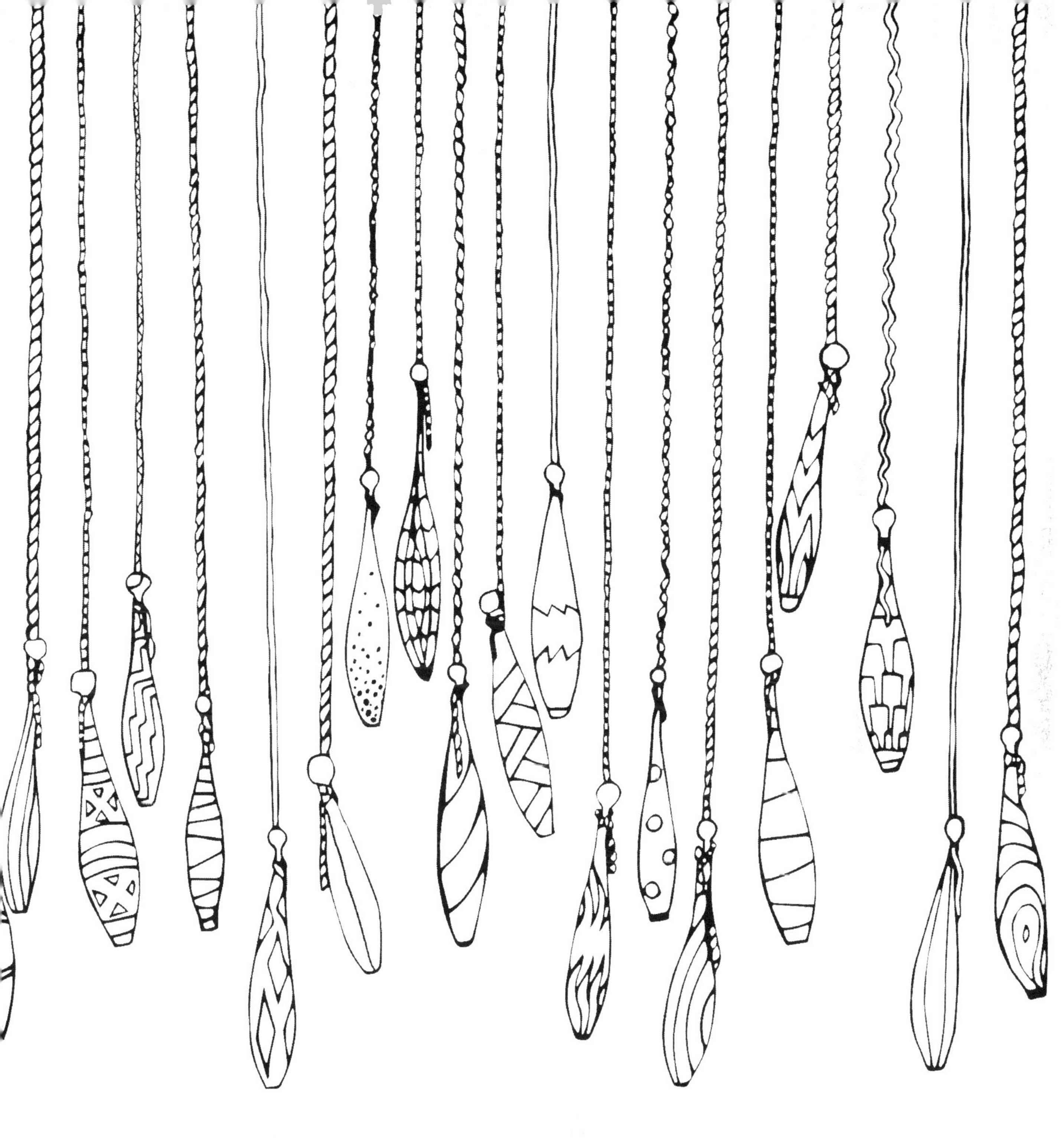

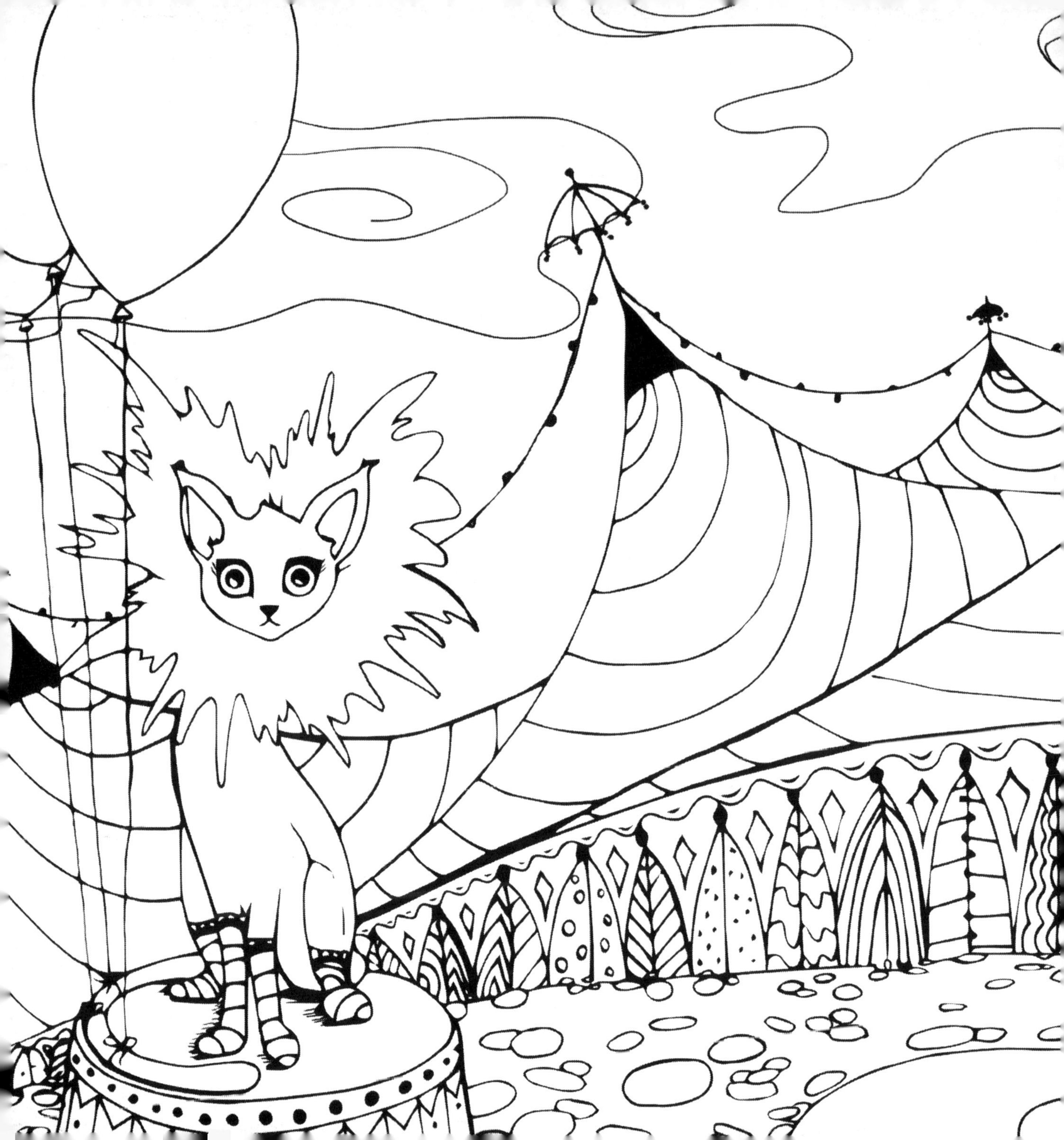

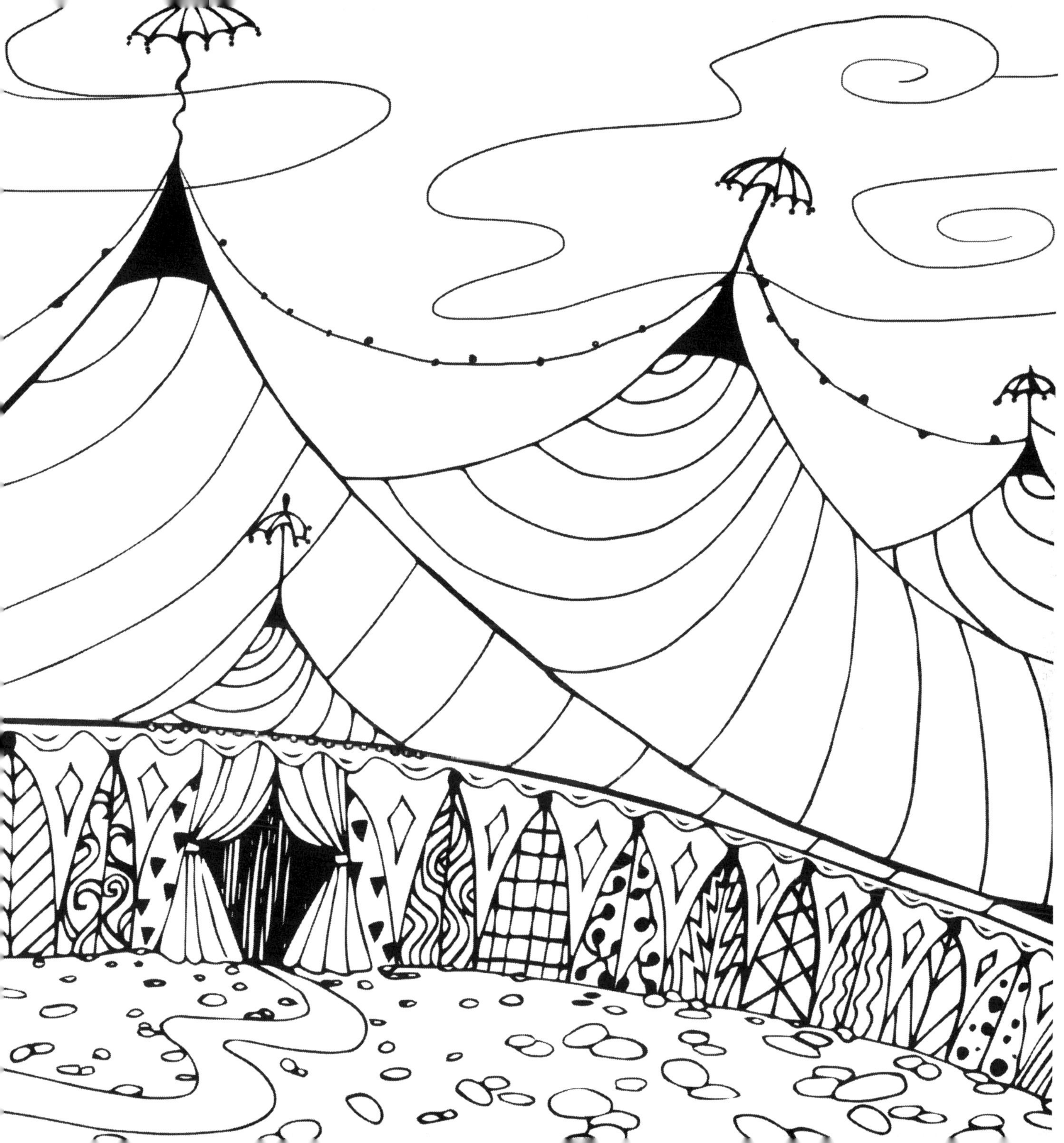

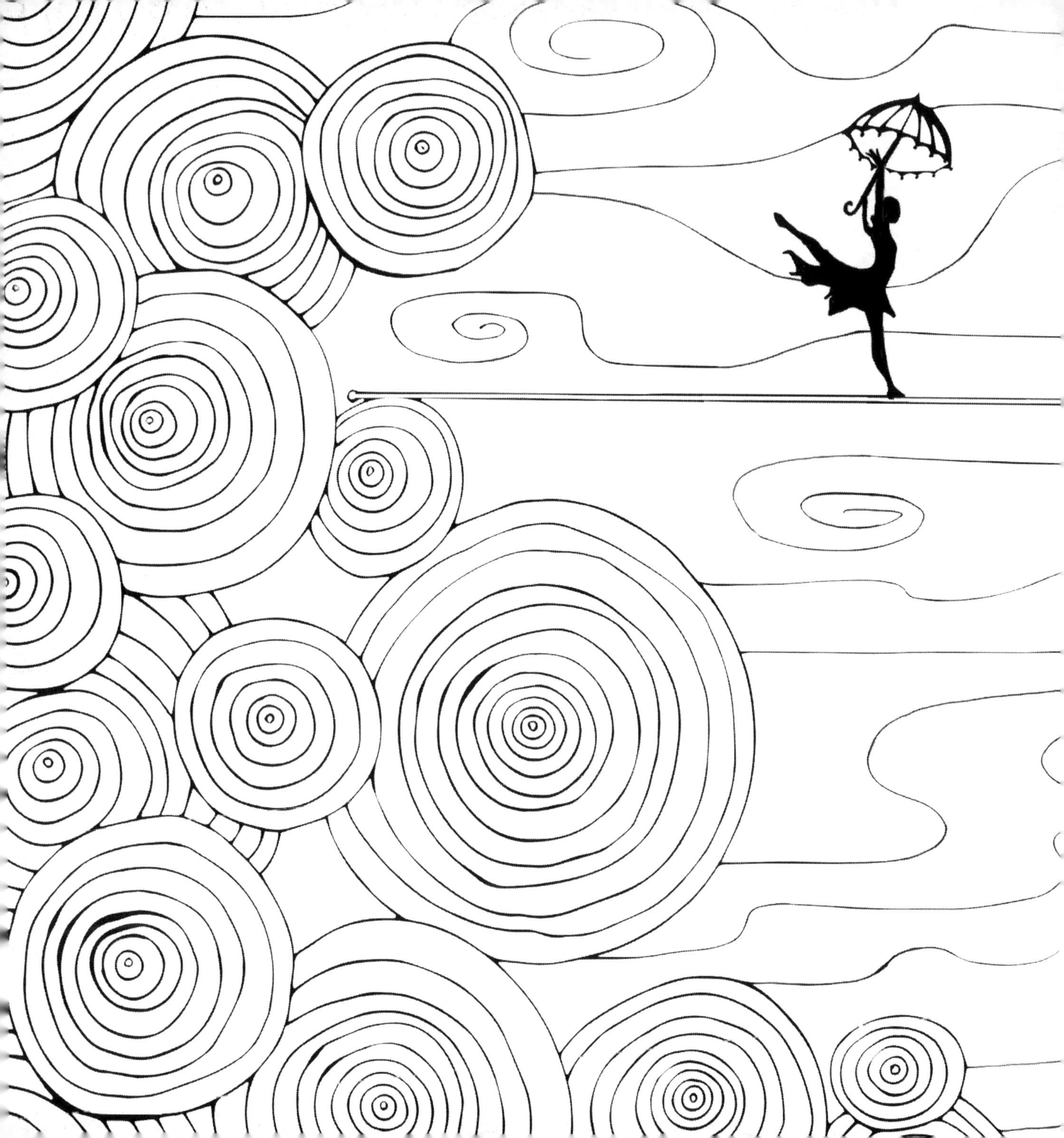

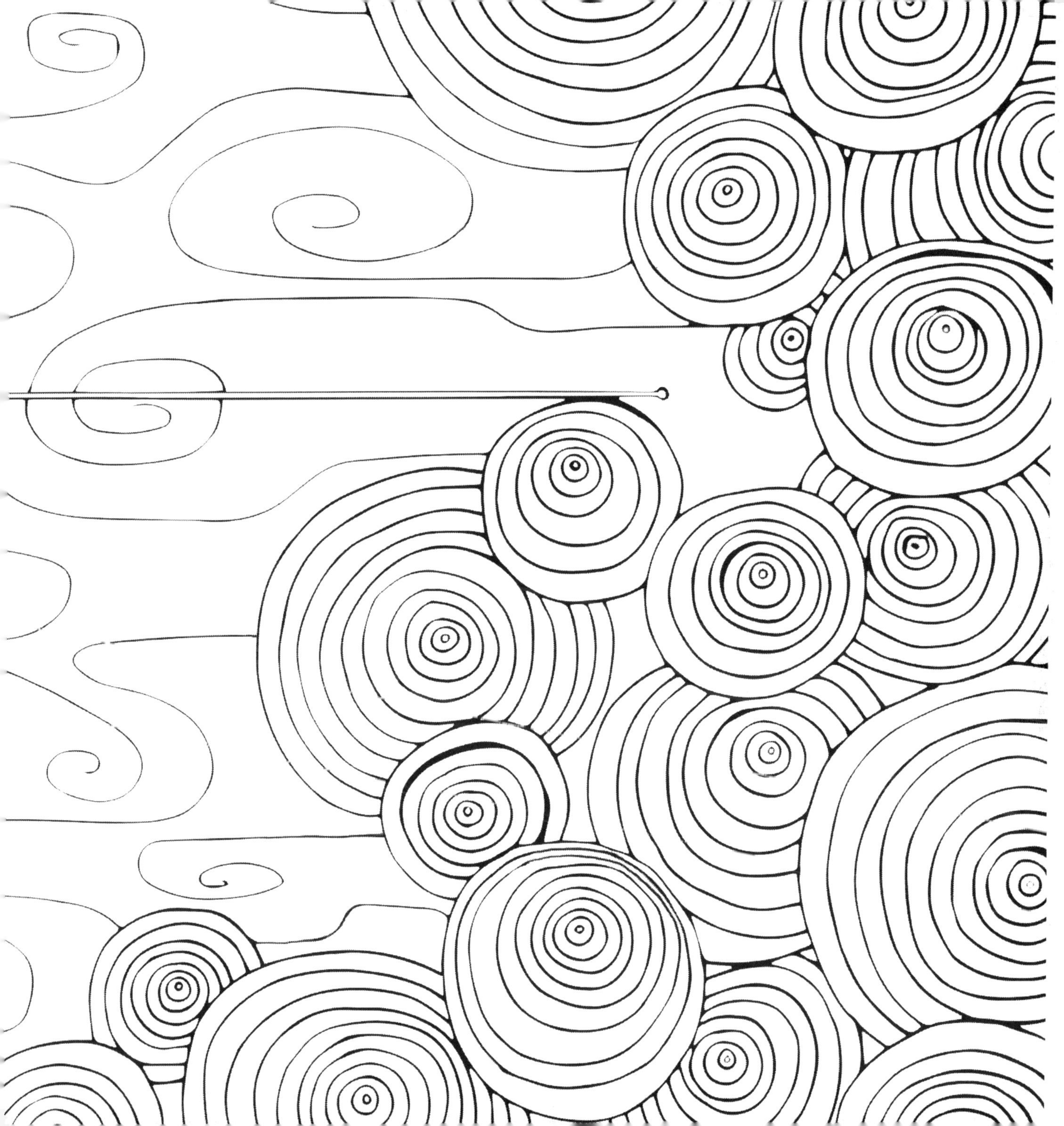

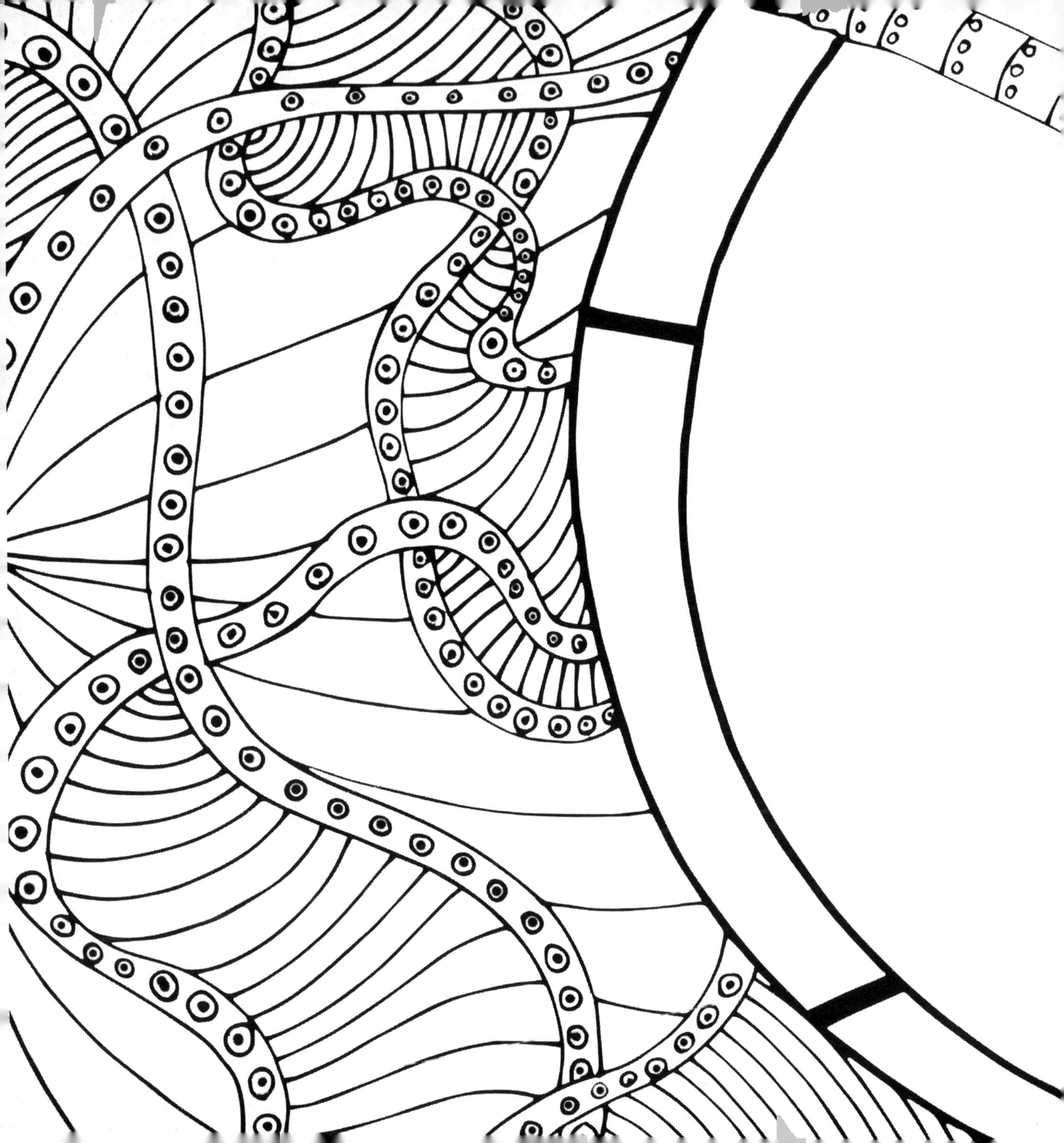

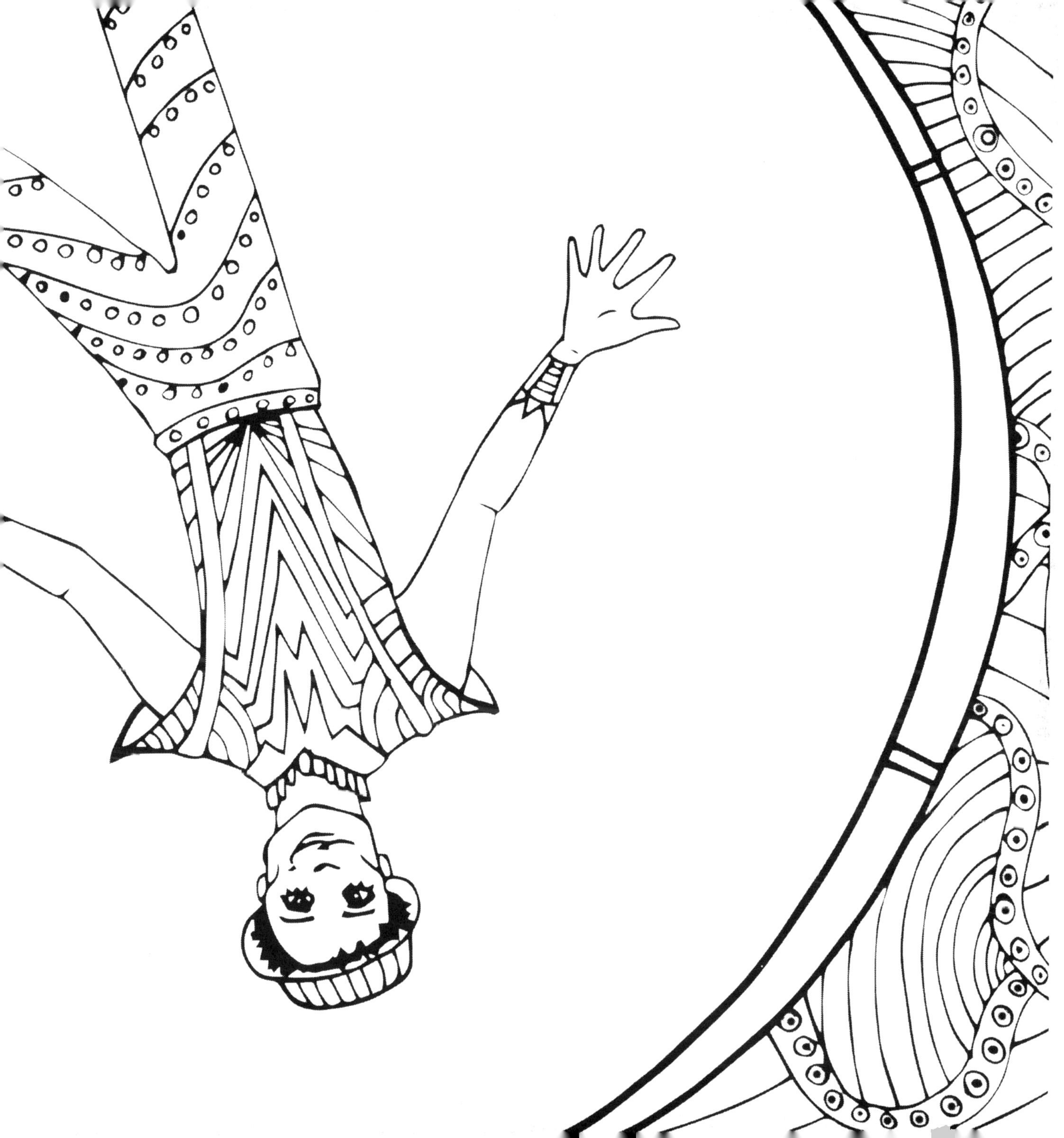

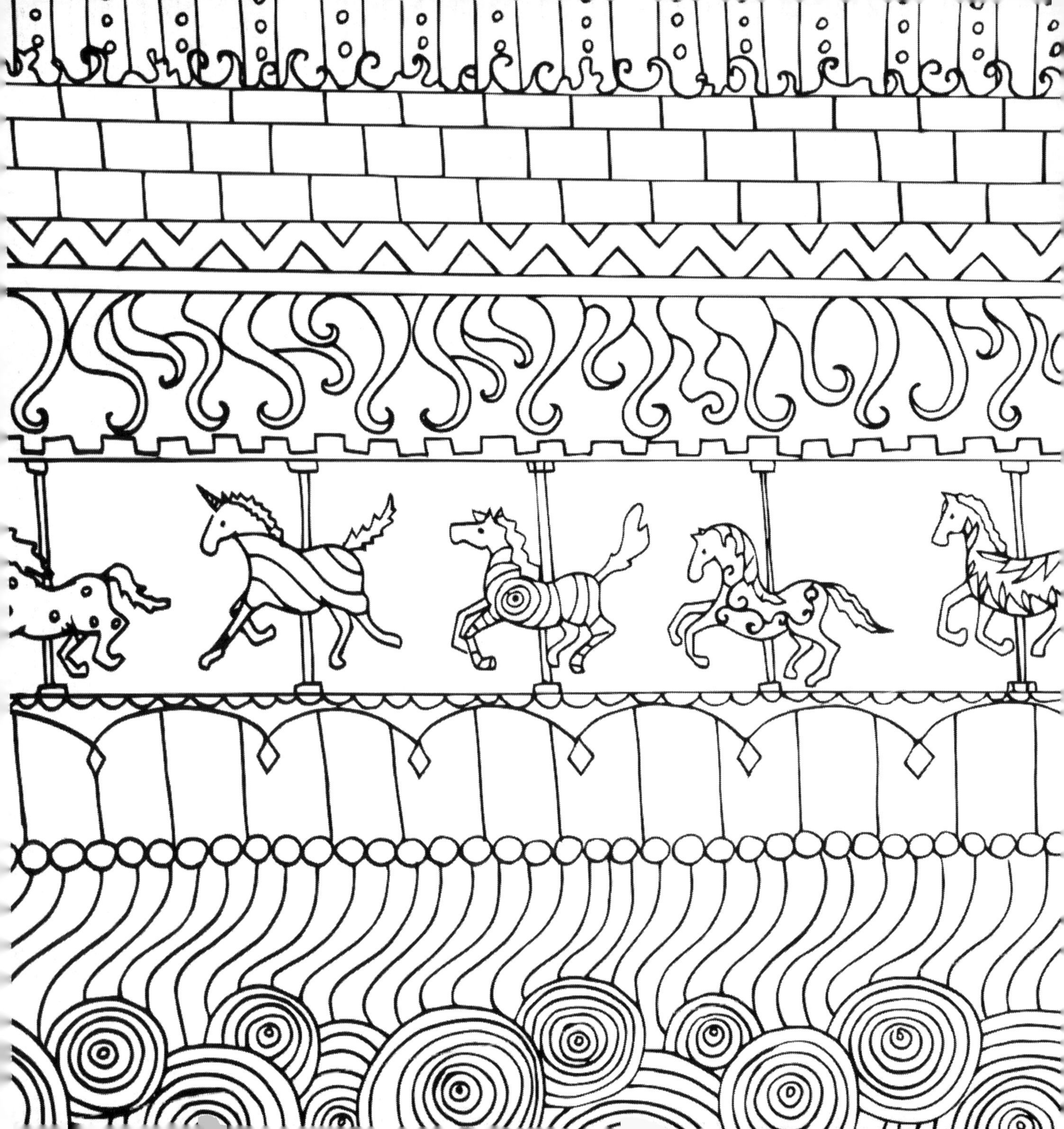

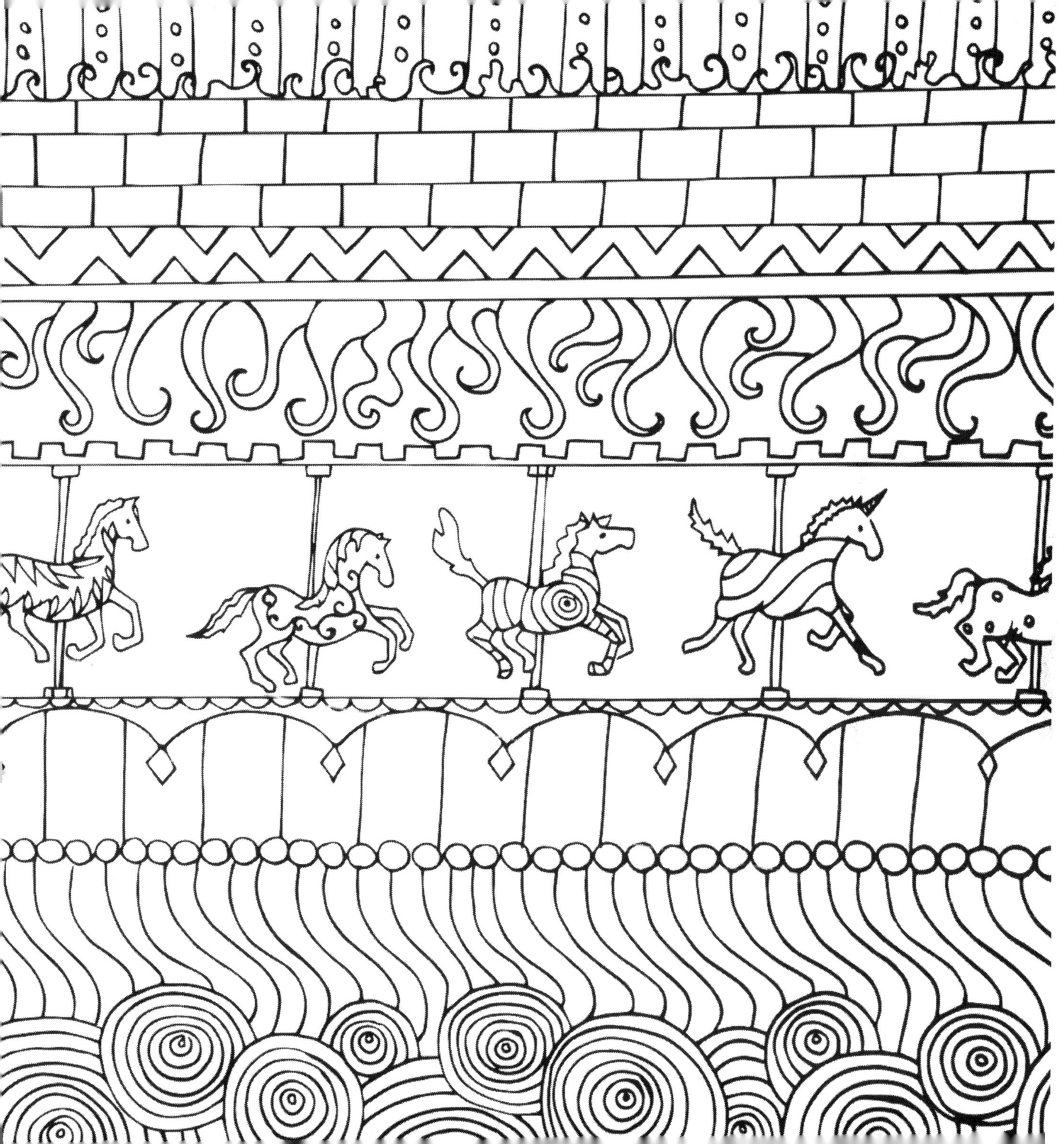

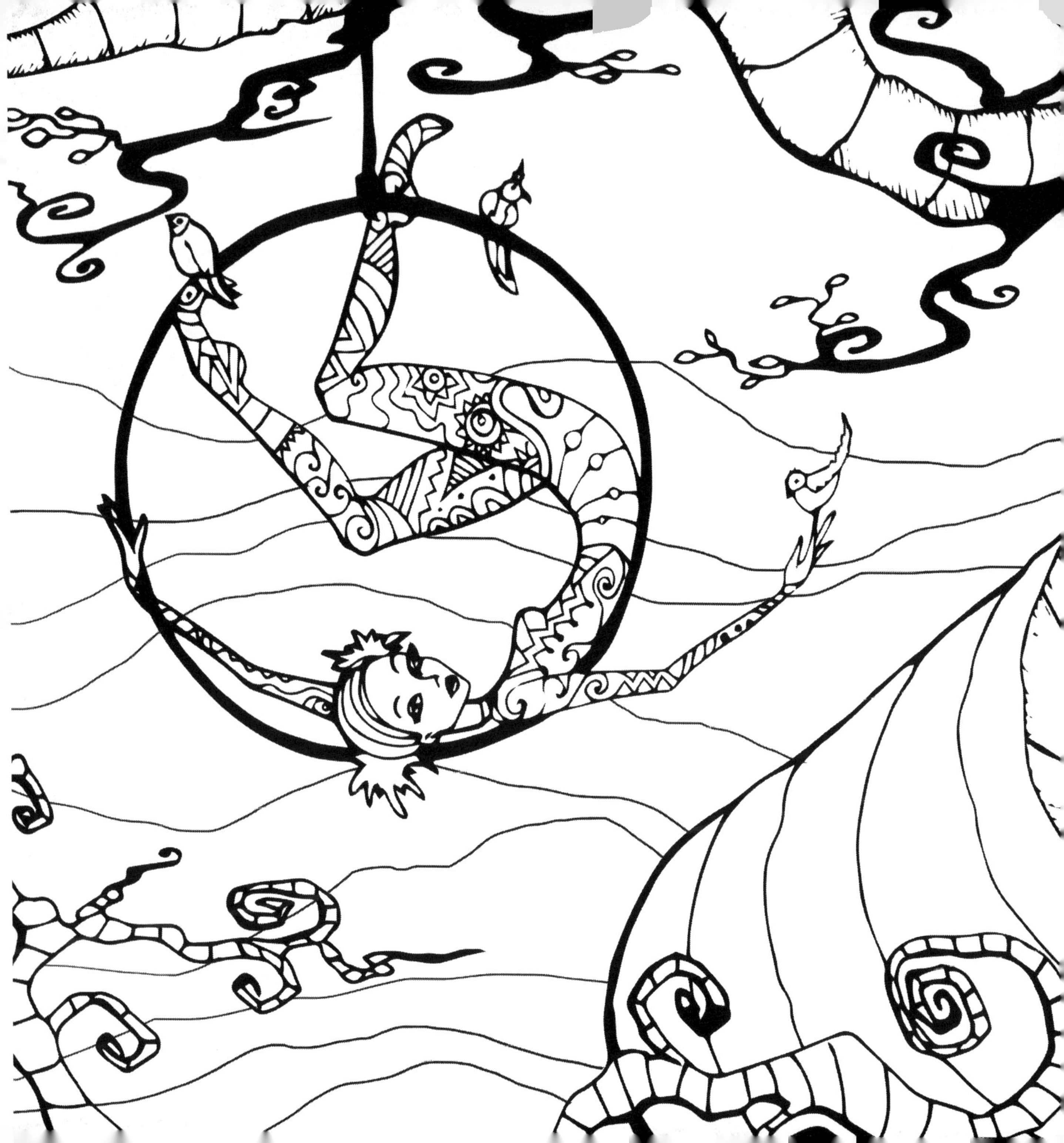

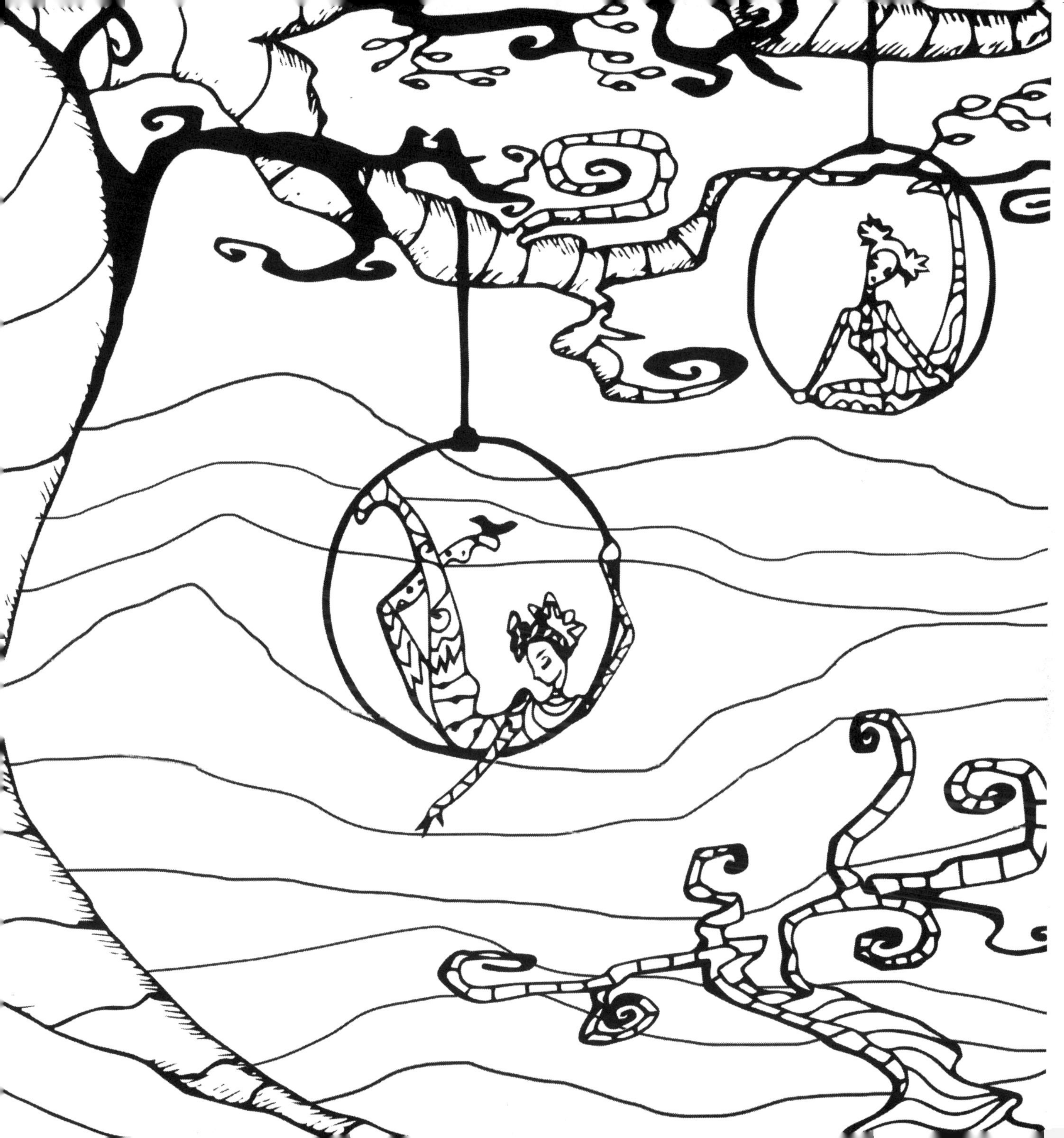

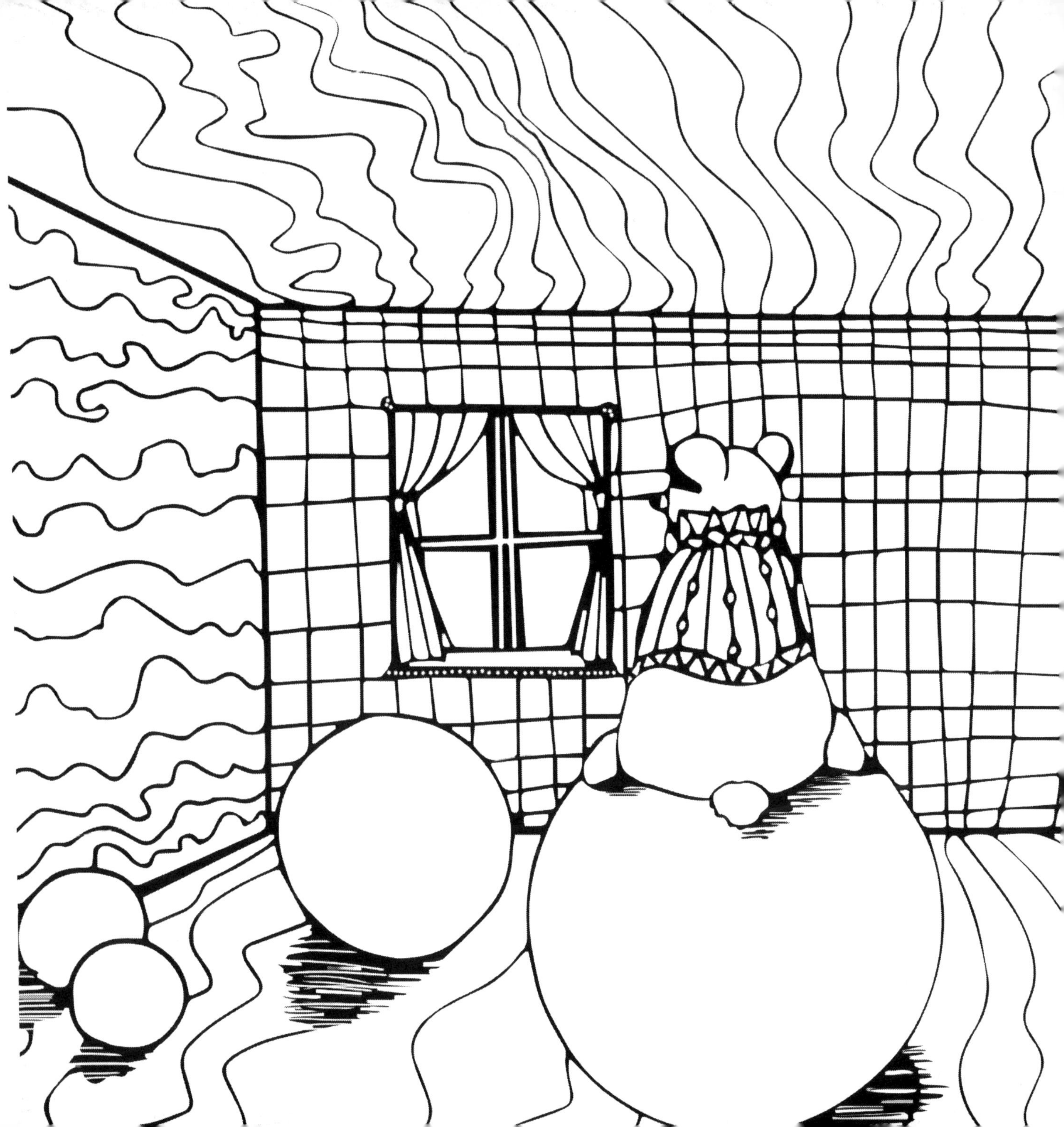

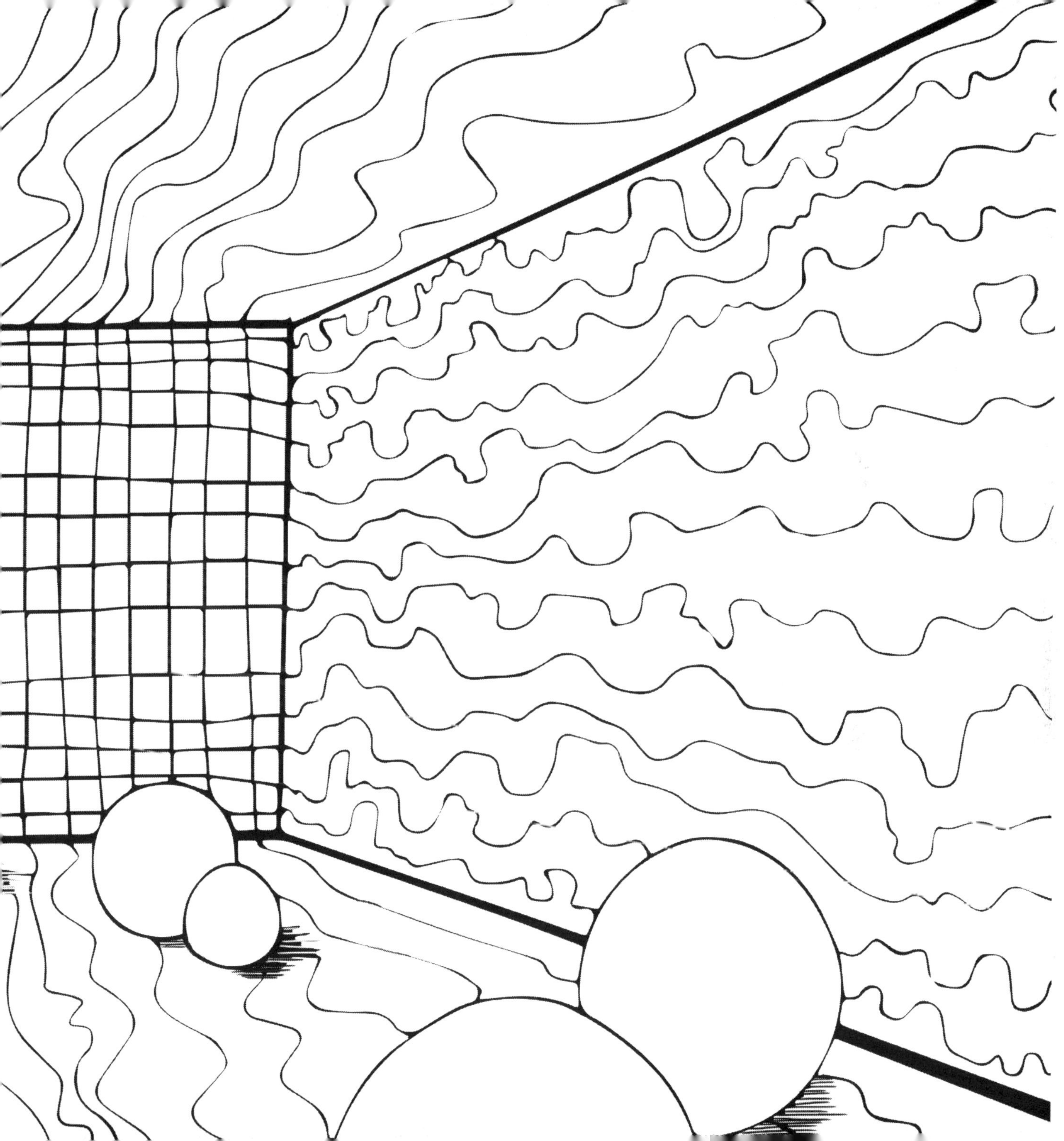

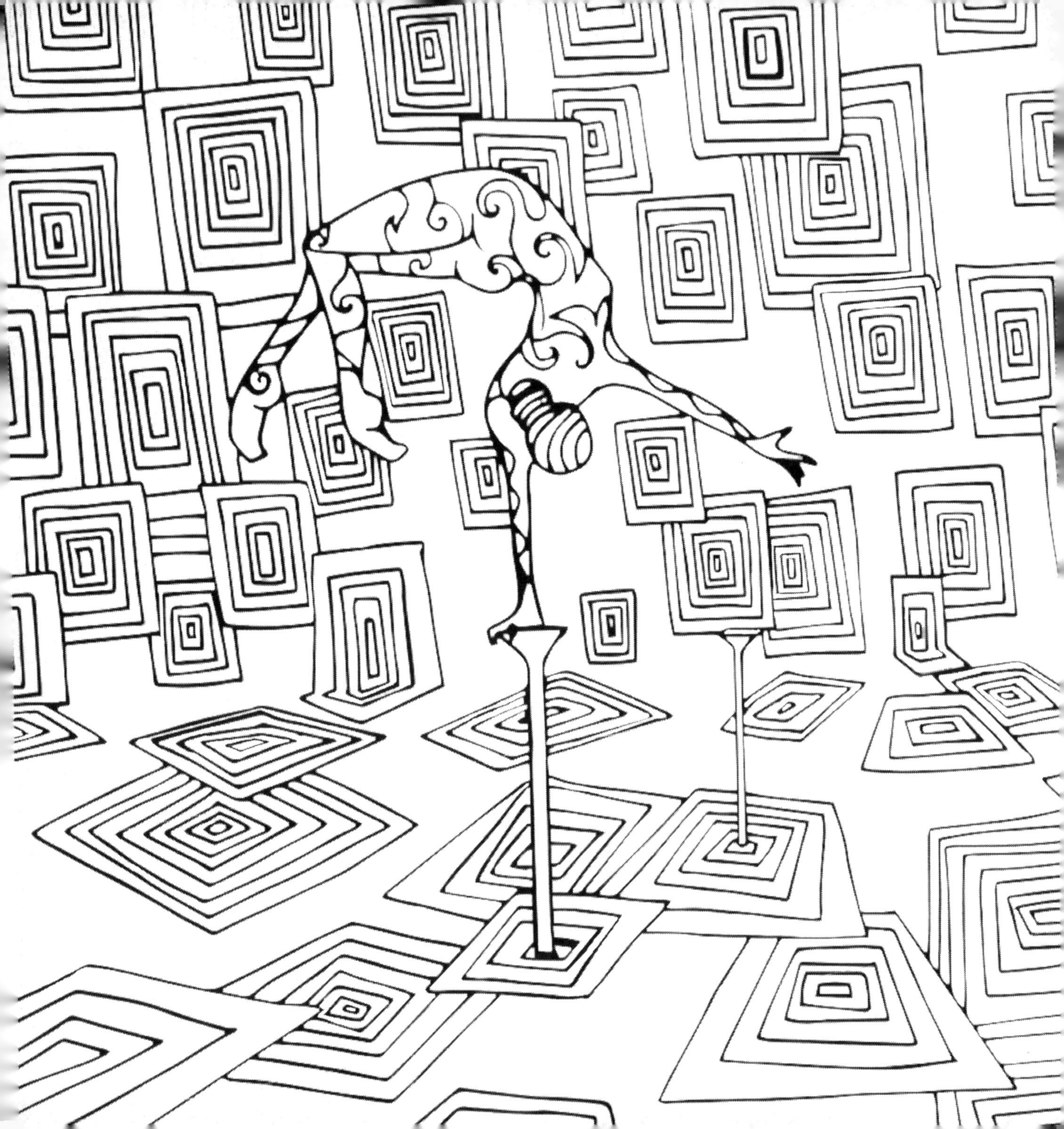

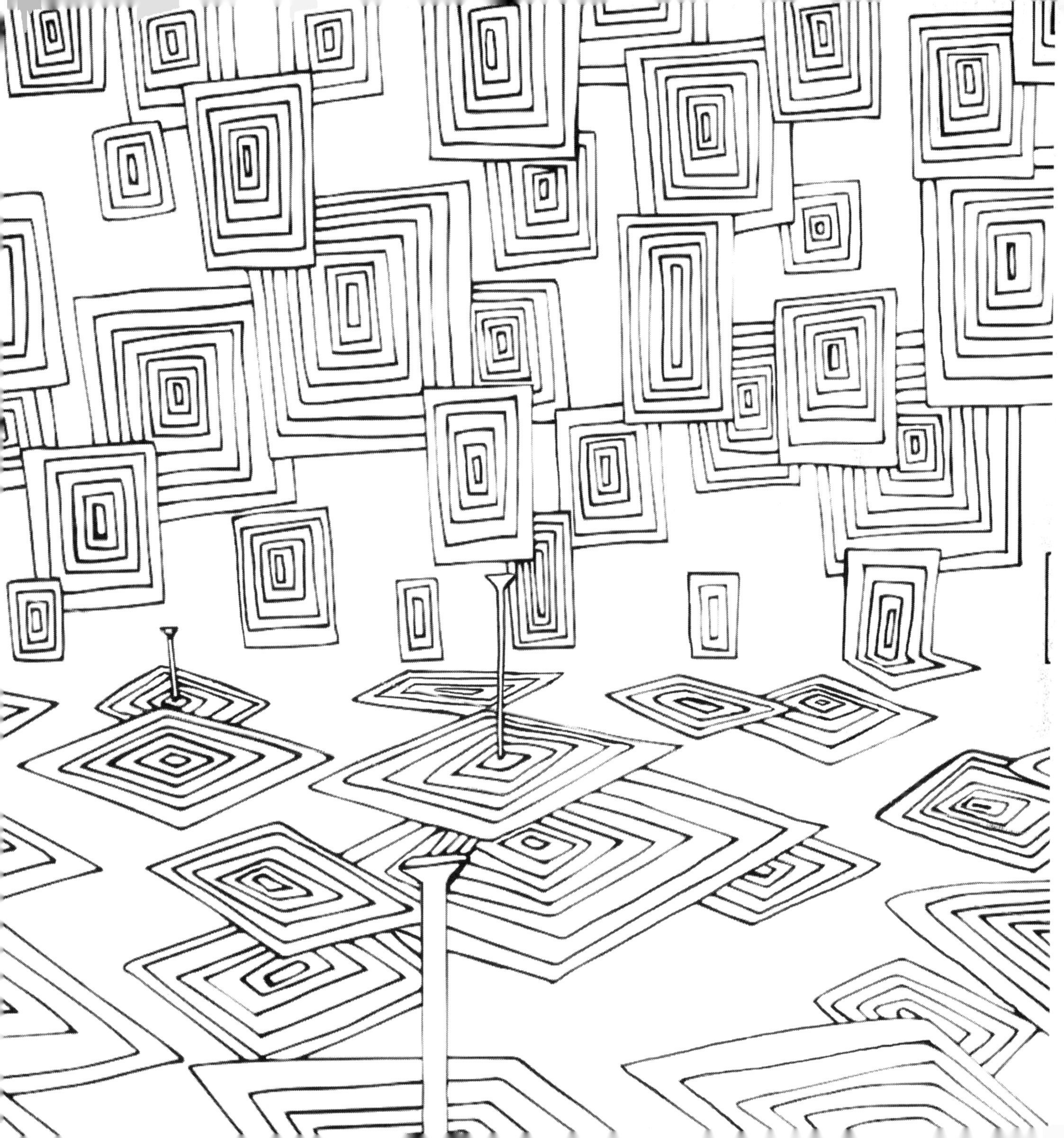

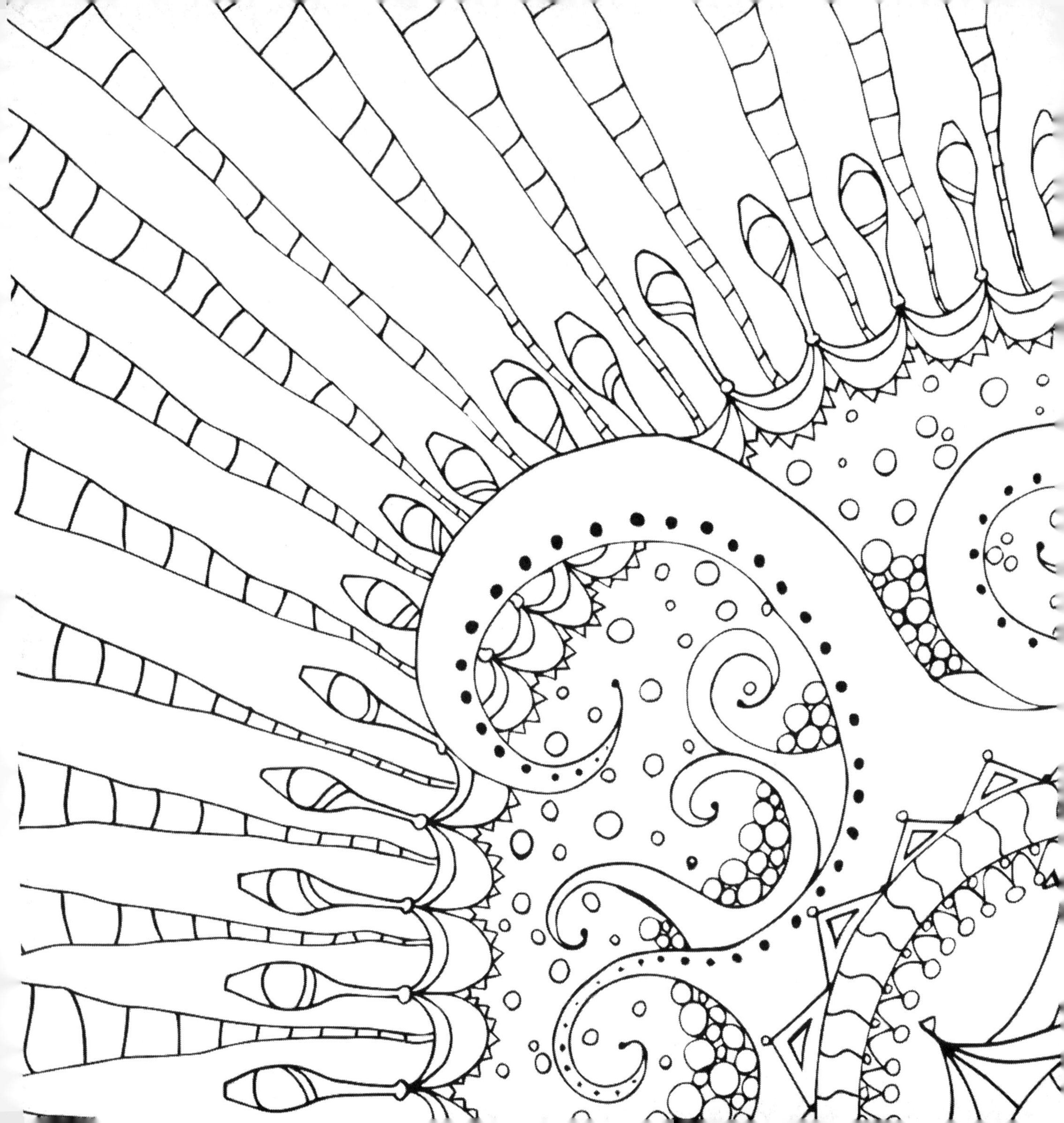

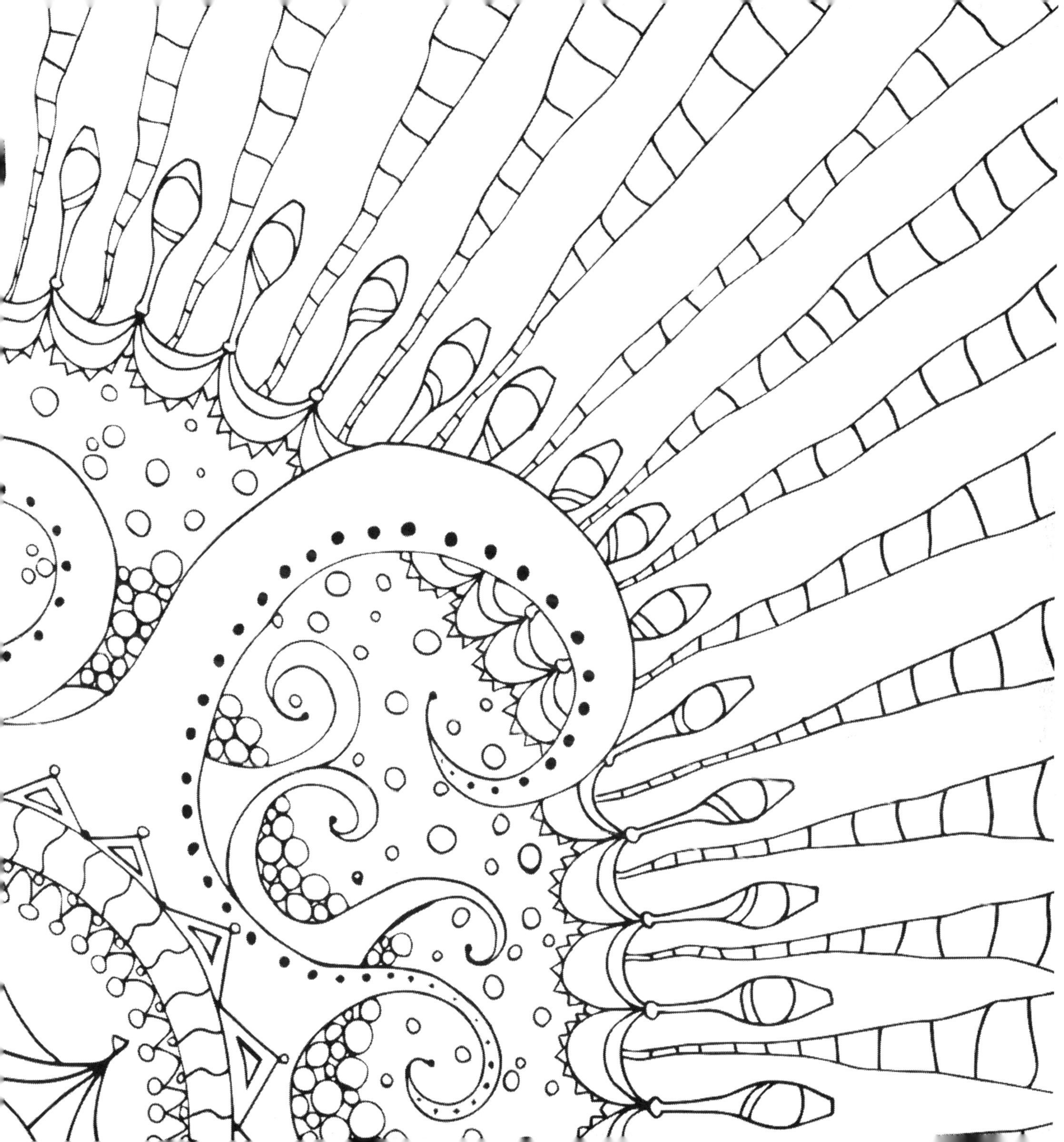

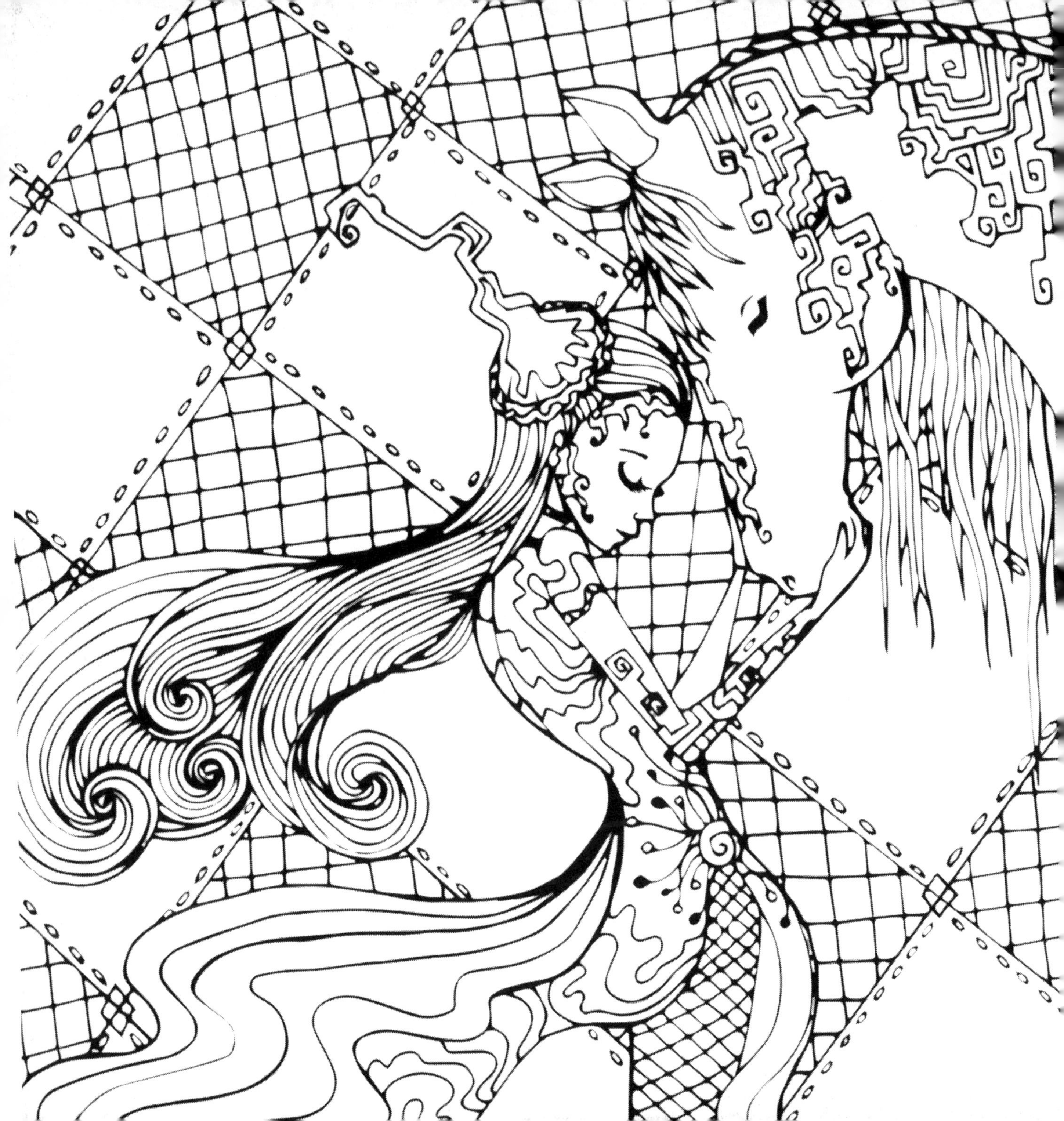

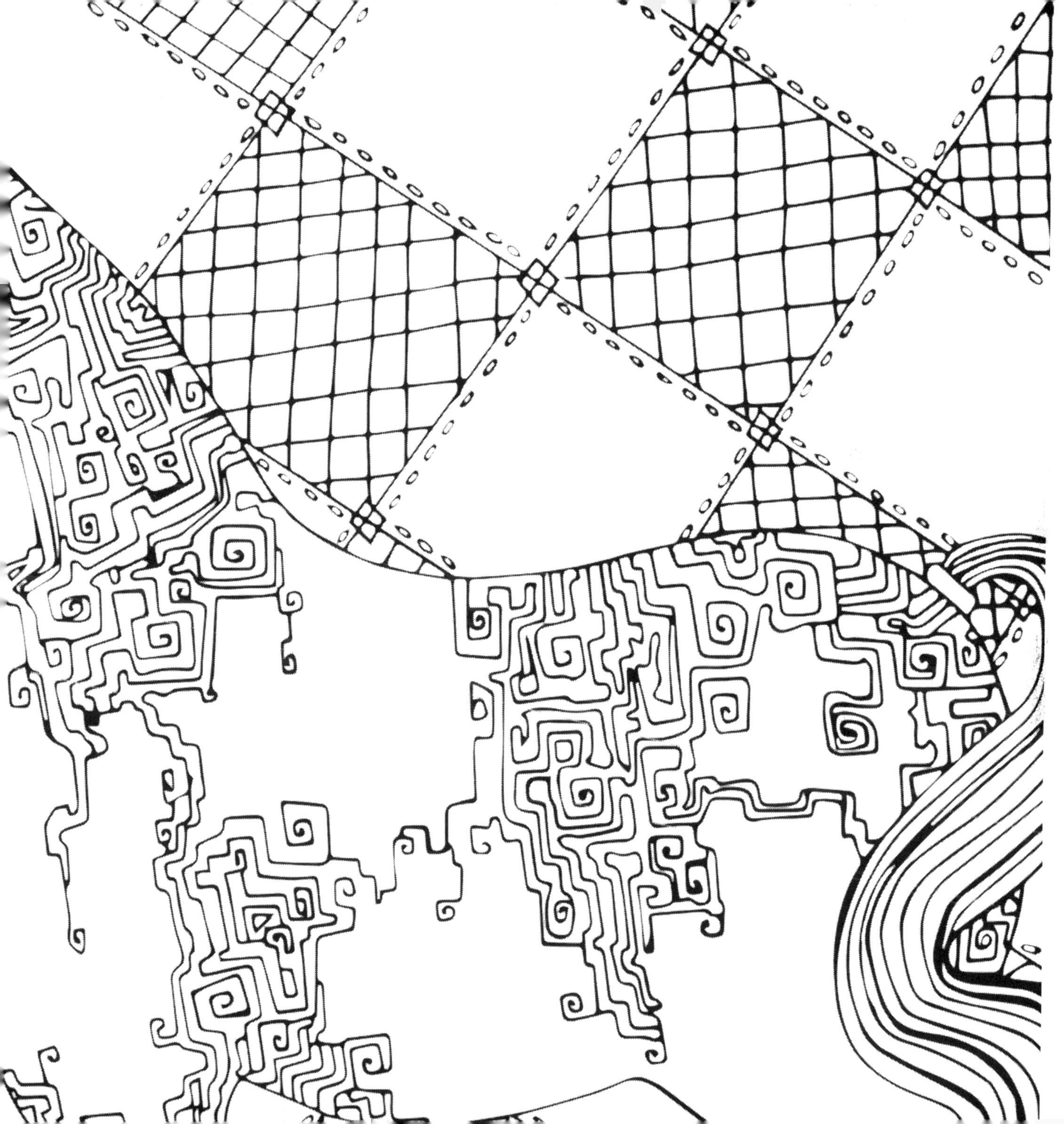

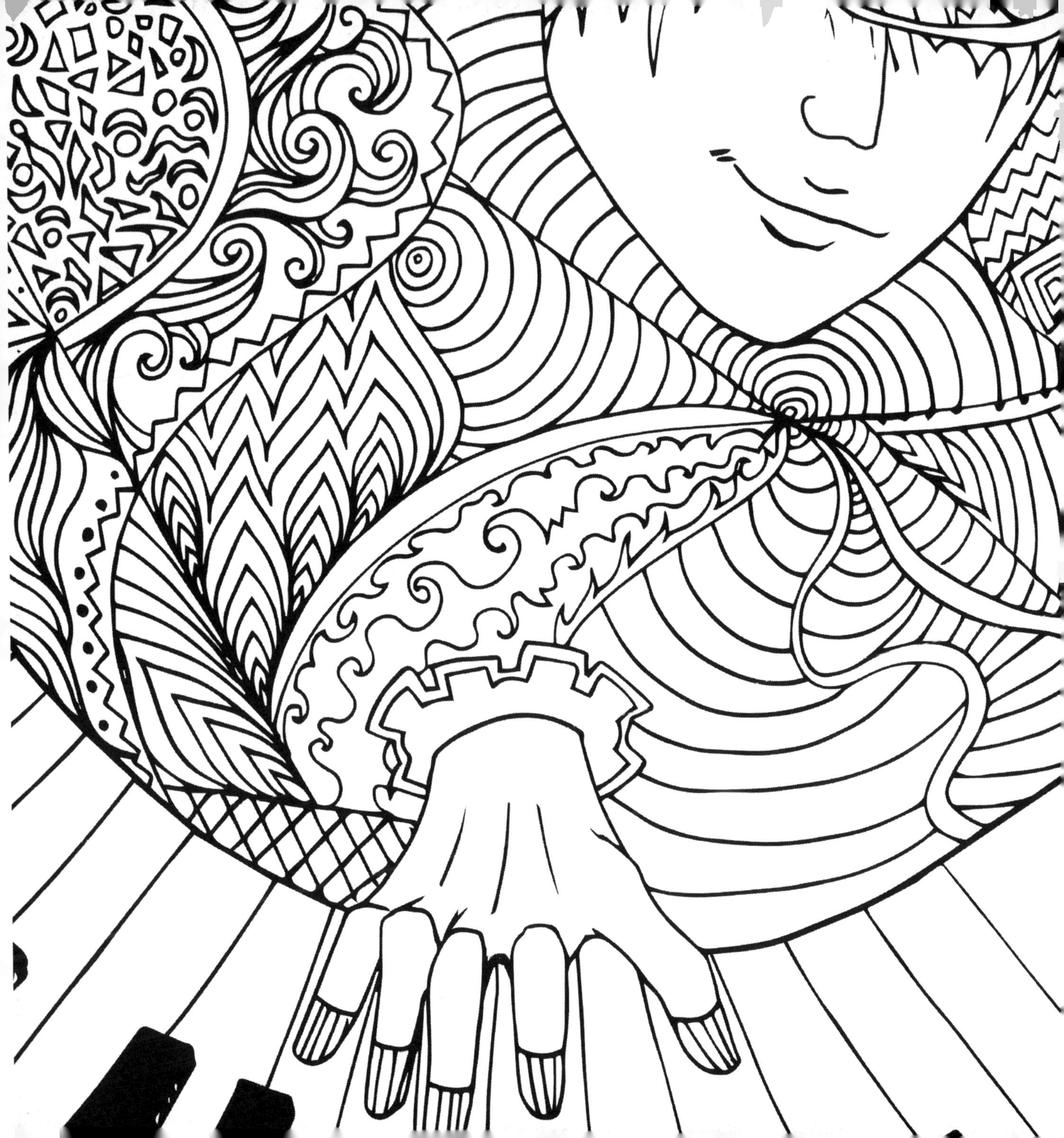

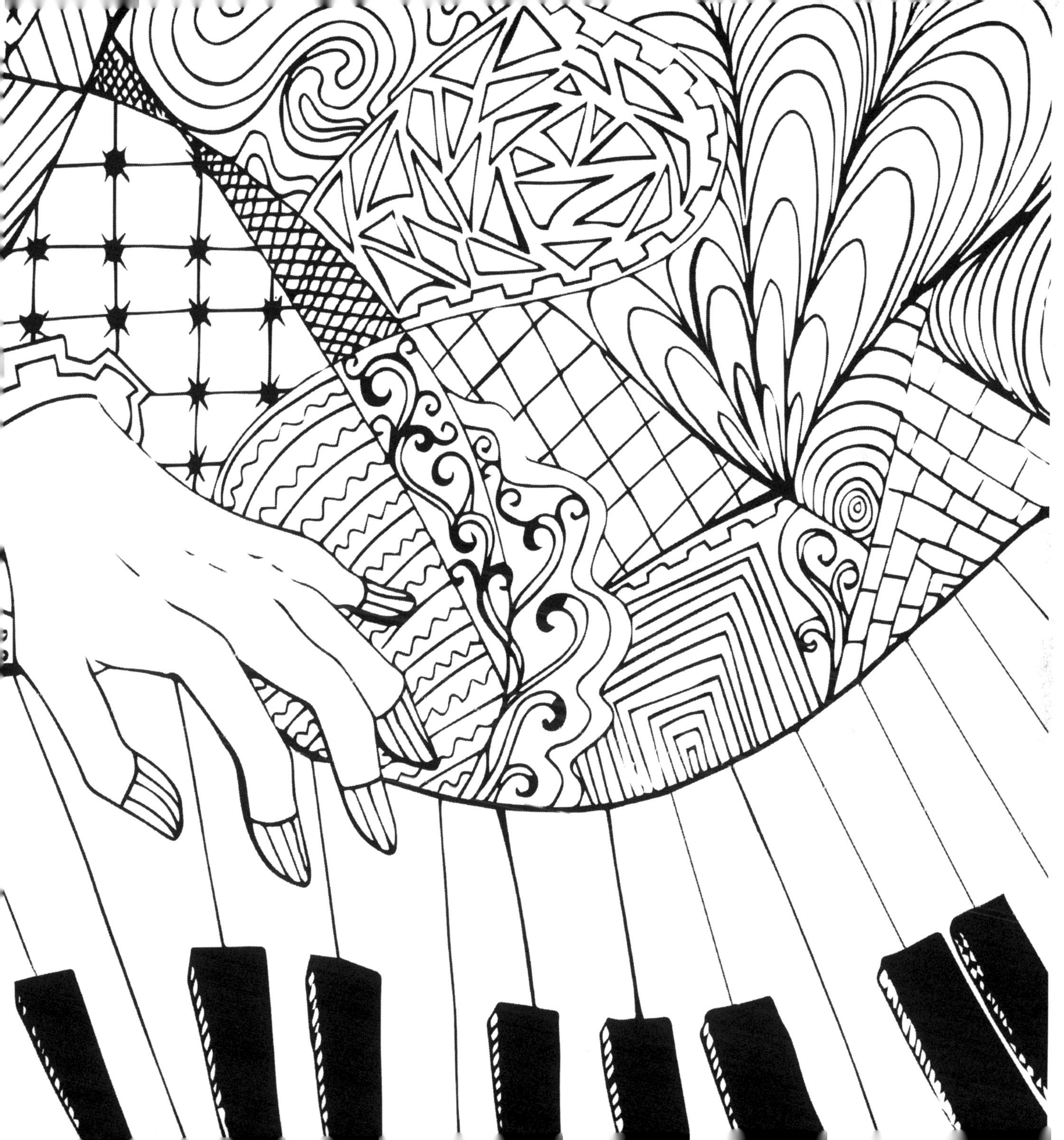

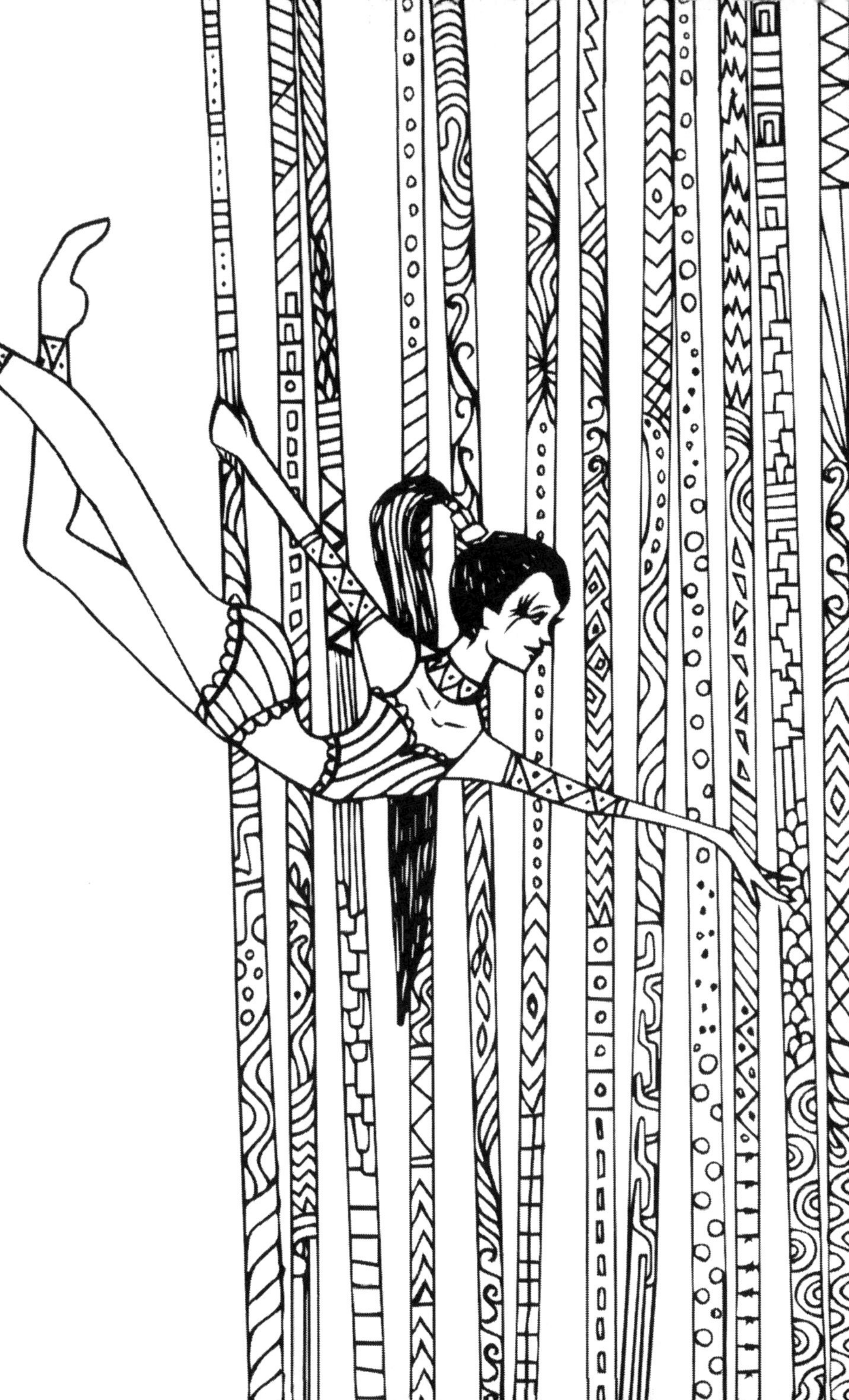

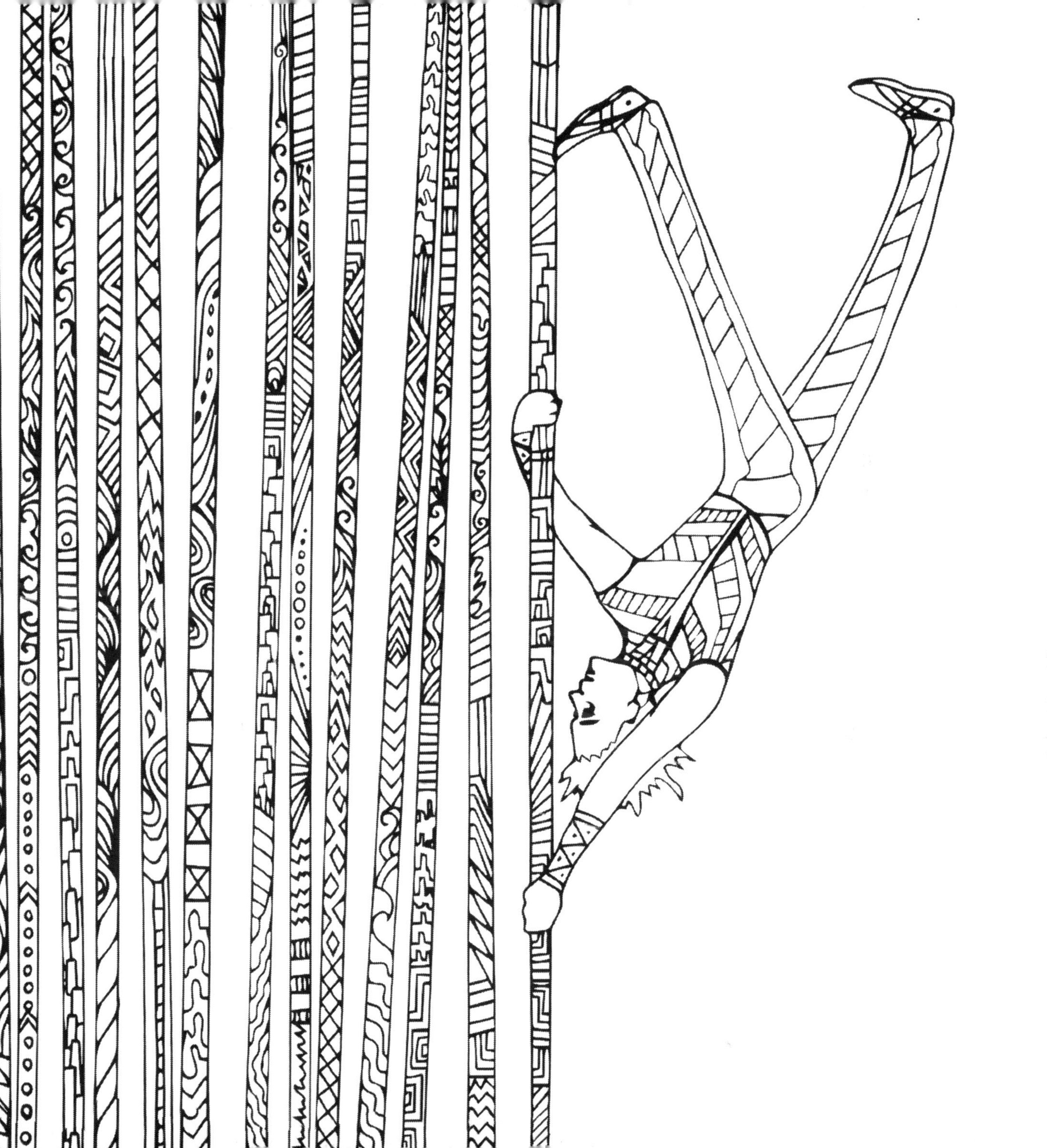

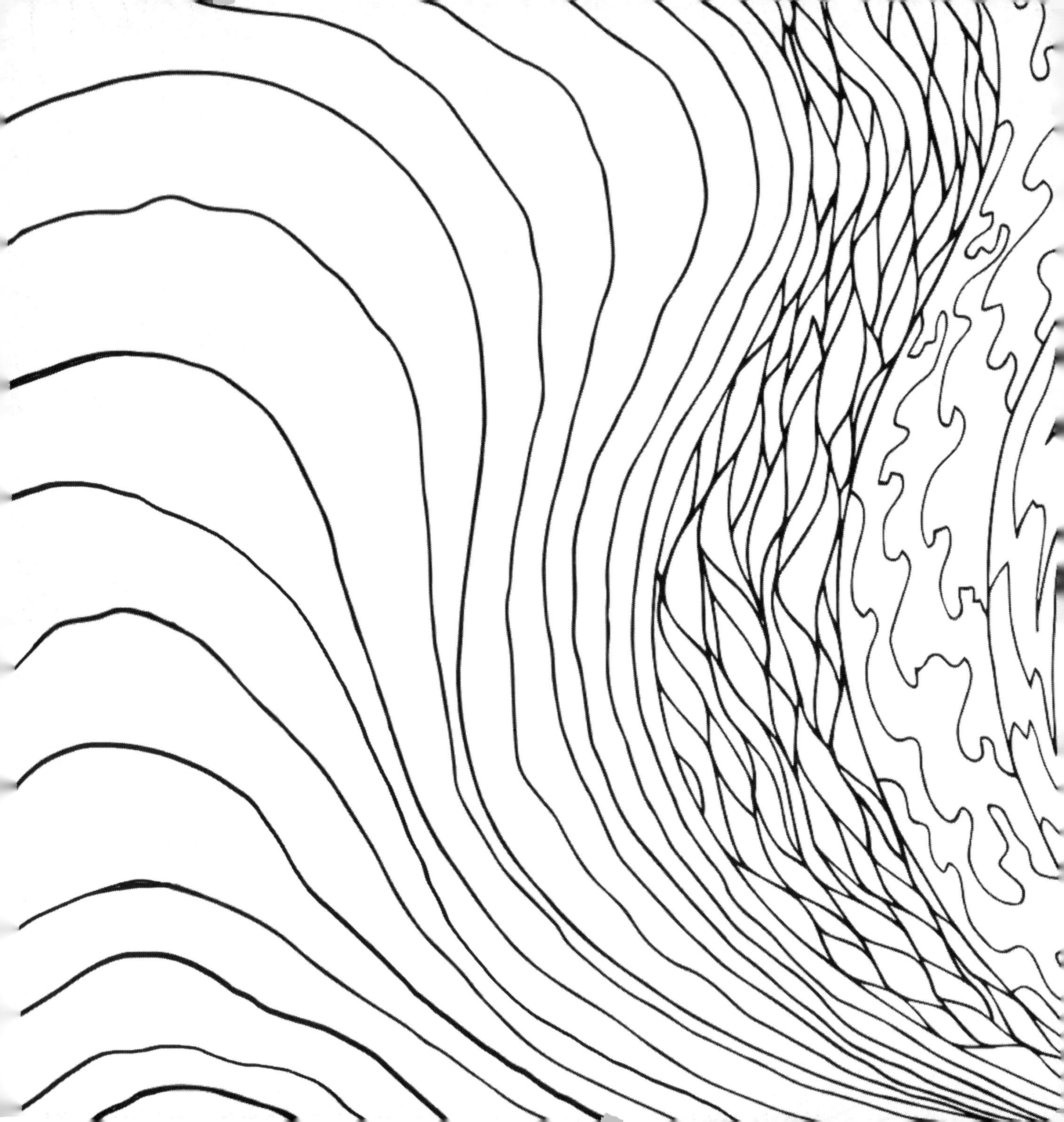

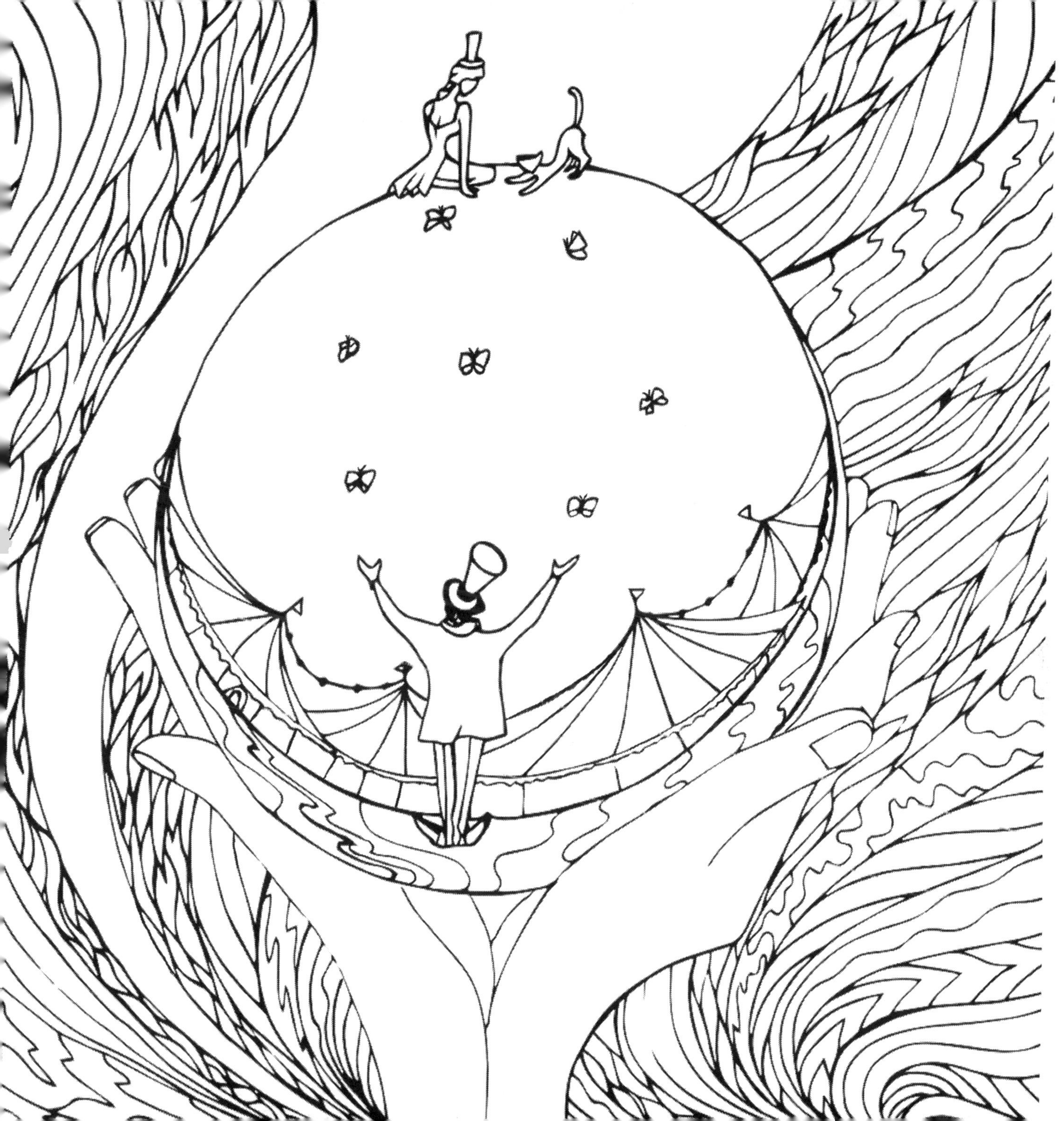

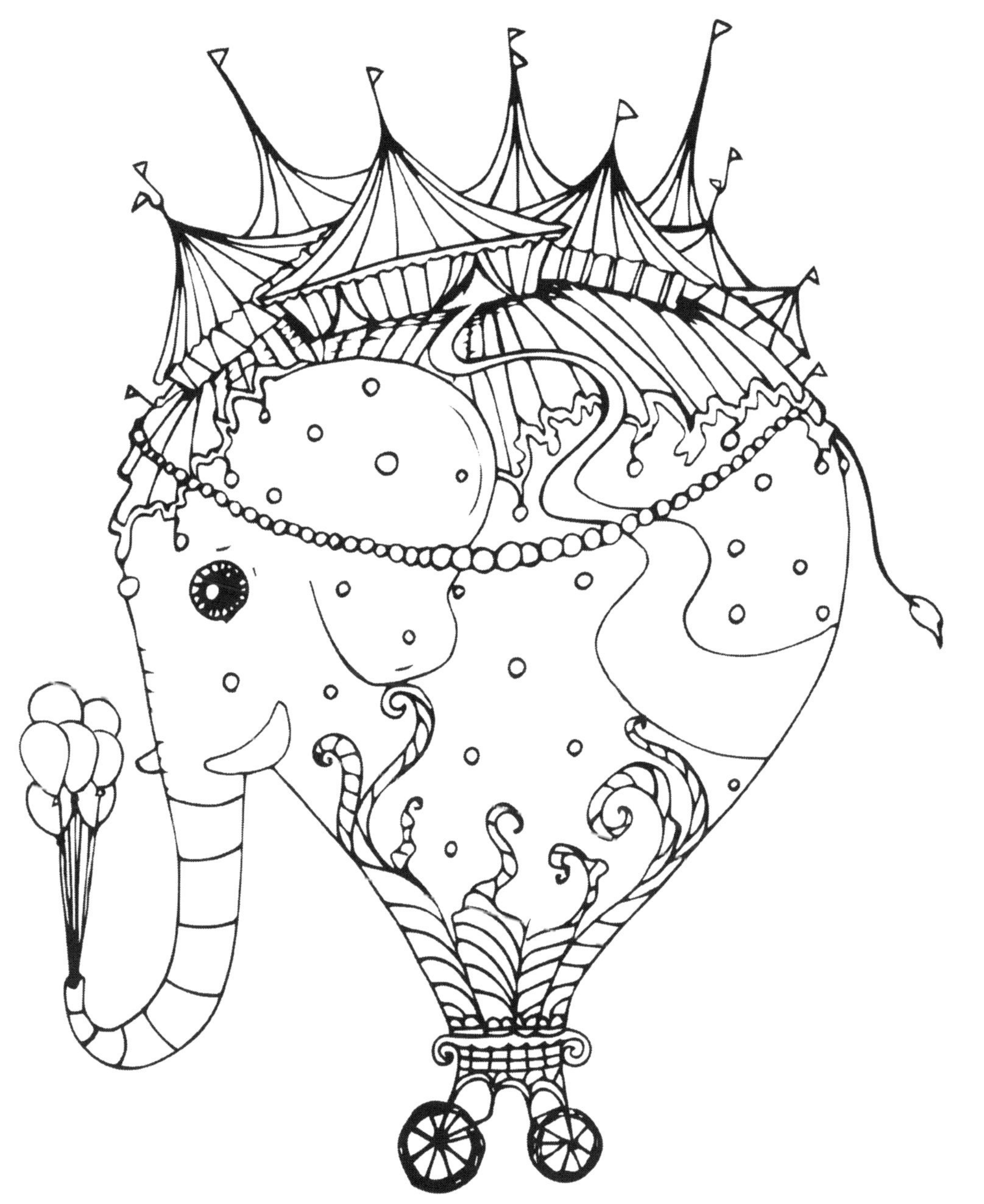

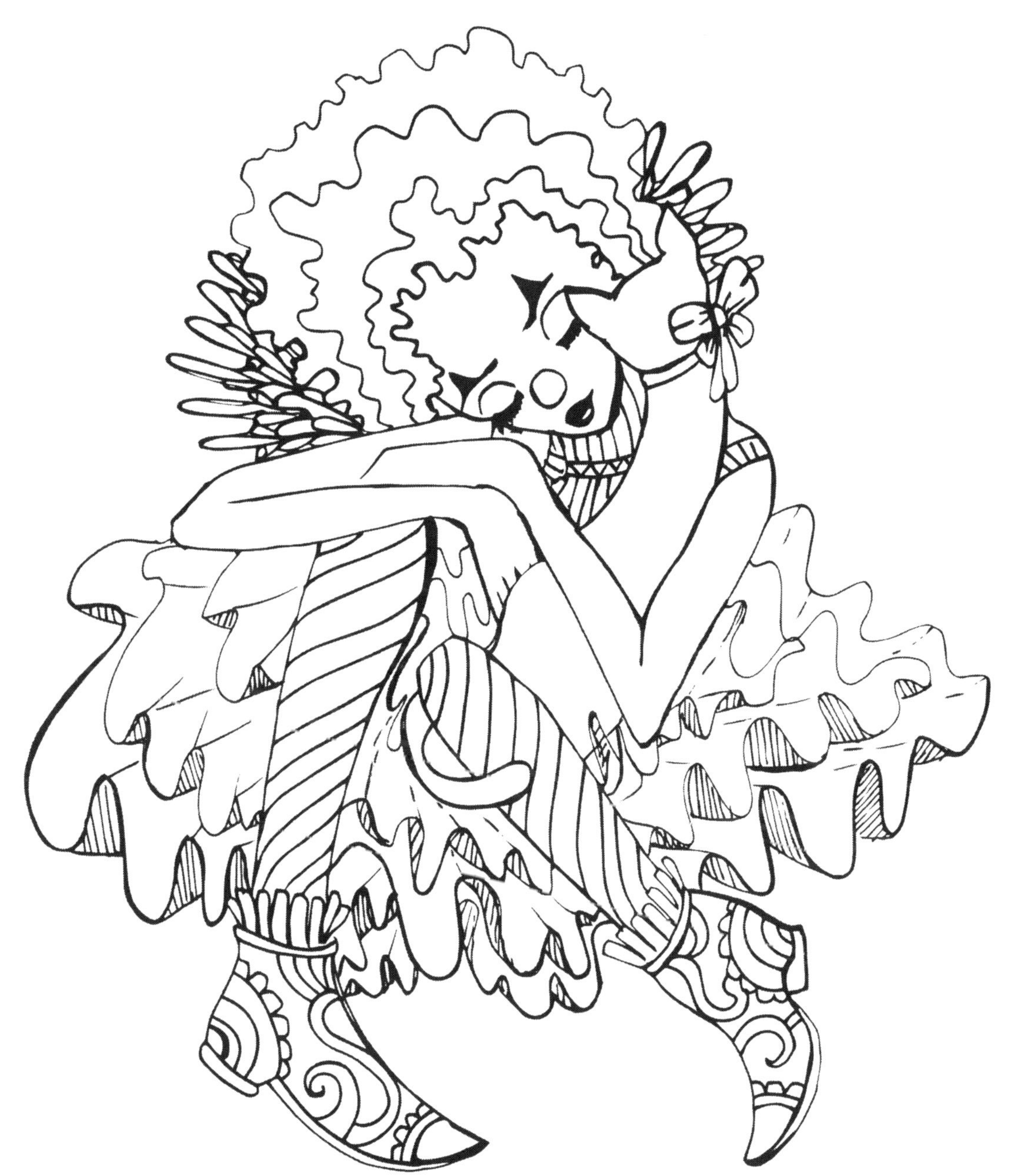

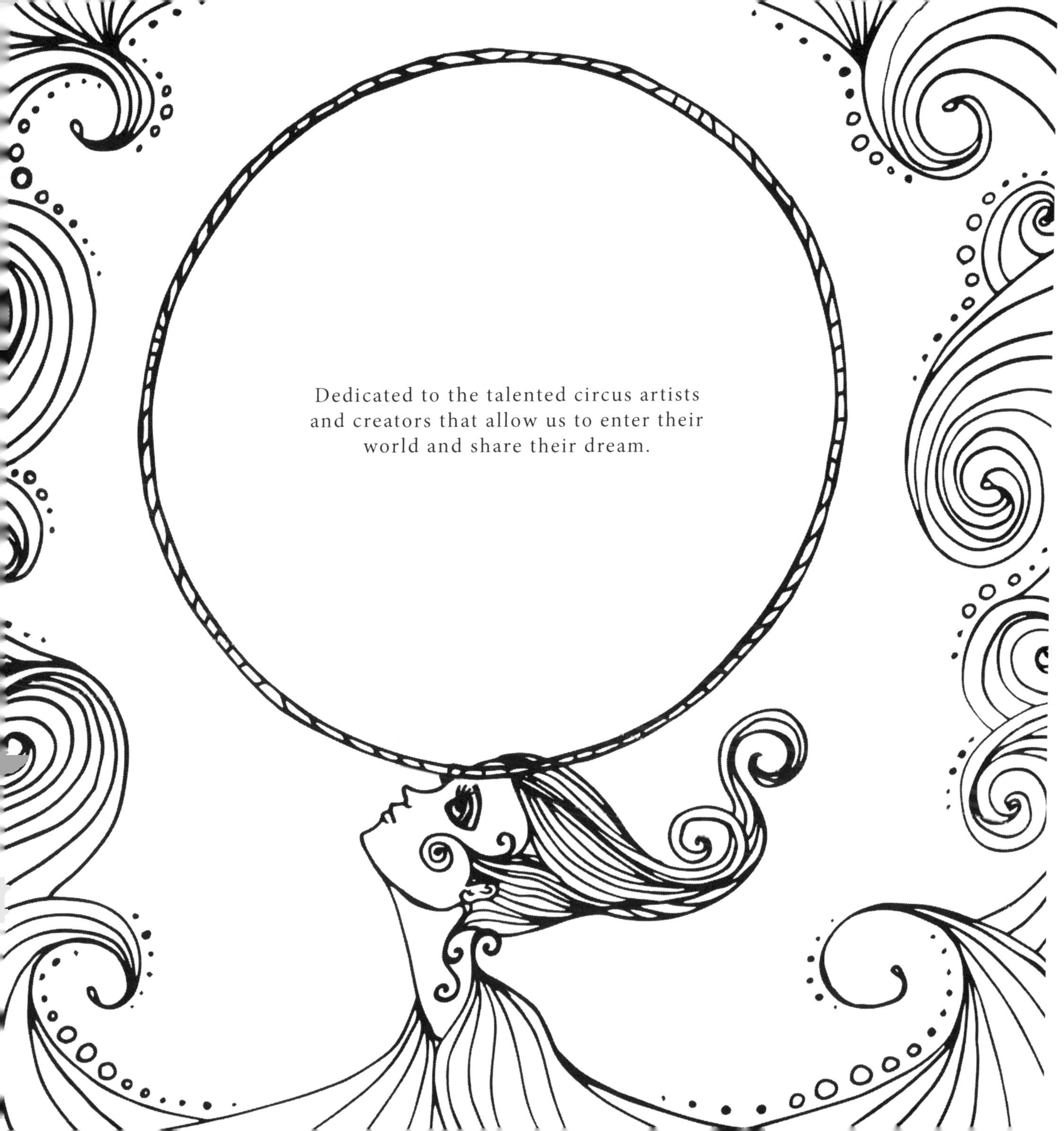

Dedicated to the talented circus artists and creators that allow us to enter their world and share their dream.

Color Experiments!

Made in the USA
Columbia, SC
23 February 2018